Curmudgeon in Corduroy

The Best of

Jerry Flemmons' Texas

Curmudgeon in

Corduroy: The Best of Jerry Flemmons' Texas

Introduction by Mike Cochran

TCU PRESS

Fort Worth

Library of Congress Cataloging-in-Publication Data

Flemmons, Jerry
    Curmudgeon in corduroy : the best of Jerry Flemmons' Texas /
introduction by Mike Cochran
    p. cm.
    "These essays were previously printed in the Fort Worth
star-telegram"—T.p. verso.
    ISBN 0-87565-217-4
    1. Texas—Social life and customs—Anecdotes. 2. Texas—Biography—
Anecdotes. 3. Texas—History—Anecdotes. I. Title: Best of
Jerry Flemmons' Texas. II. Title.

F386.6 .F58 2000
976.4—dc21
                                            99-057071

These essays were previously printed in the *Fort Worth Star-Telegram* and *Southern Living*.

Cover art by J. D. Crowe
Design by Barbara Whitehead

Contents

Introduction

A true challenge, this. As I write, Jerry Flemmons, my long-time friend, colleague, and confidant, is only a few days dead. Jerry's heart medicine conspired with an insidious cancer and a stroke to finally kill him in a Houston hospital. "Cheated death again," he would chuckle after each deadly encounter of his last decade. But not this time. His defiance of the odds ended at age sixty-three. This terrible sadness, shared with Jerry's family and many friends and admirers, will surely pass. But with us forever will be memories of Jerry's grumpy charm and indomitable spirit, his passion for a story well told and his compassion for the people and places about which he wrote so eloquently.

Which brings us to the good part, the happy part, that part of which is in fact called *The Best of Jerry Flemmons' Texas*. The actual title of course is *Curmudgeon in Corduroy*, but this final collection of Jerry's essays showcases the full range of his bountiful writing talents and his affection for all things Texan. Jerry was nothing if not a skilled, prolific journalist, and often he was at his best when writing about Texas and Texans. He seldom admitted it, but he loved Texas and Fort Worth and spurned a lifetime of invitations to abandon either or both. With his sly wit and delicate touch, Jerry chronicled our triumphs and traumas, poked gentle fun at our shortcomings, and shamelessly embraced our outrageous mythology.

"Aggrandizement is an old Texas habit, though I, as many others, believe that the state really is larger than life," Jerry confessed in an introduction to *Texas Siftings,* one of several of his earlier books published by TCU Press. "Texas," Jerry insisted, "is myth-sized and deserving of the exaggerations we have bestowed on it over the years."

Until his purported "retirement" in 1997, Jerry spent more than three decades as an often-honored writer for the *Fort Worth Star-Telegram.* He was recognized nationally as one of the top travel writers in America, but he was so much more. His early reporting on the Kennedy assassination and the University of Texas tower sniper are almost legendary around the *Star-Telegram.* So was his later masterpiece on the killer tornado in Wichita Falls. Back then, as a contemporary at The Associated Press, I often caught Jerry's act up close and personal. It was always educational, but, more importantly, it was also inspirational. Our mutual friend Mike Blackman, the retired executive editor and vice president of the *Star-Telegram,* recalled a day or so ago the comments Jerry made at a staff conference in 1968. His words reveal the heart and soul of a writer's writer.

"That day in the conference room," Mike wrote, "Jerry spoke generously about the love of the language, the art of listening and how the selection of the right words builds good sentences, which build good paragraphs, which build good stories, which should always have a beginning, a middle and an end. He spoke about cadence and rhythm, about making the words work for you rather than the other way around. He talked about building drama and how crucial the ear is to the telling of a story. He talked about timing, how and when to introduce new elements into a story, timing being everything. At the end, he said, "If I can ever help, come find me." Many of us did.

As the very first writer-in-residence at Tarleton State University, where he once was a star quarterback, Jerry continued to produce his popular and eminently readable weekly opinion columns for the *Star-Telegram*. It is the best of his provocative newspaper essays that appear here for the first time in book form. So come along as Jerry reminds us again of the gravity of black-eyed peas and cornbread on New Year's Day, the ecstasy of real chicken-fried steak, the autumnal mysteries of Frito Pie, the societal virtue of front porches, and the versatility of cowboy hats. In a flash he whisks us to Austin circa 1966, atop the crimson-stained tower where "Charles Joseph Whitman lay in the shadow of his last afternoon." Or to the Ozarks, late at night, with the air smelling of hickory wood smoke from an open fire. A girl's voice, he wrote, full and unaffected, came from beyond the bonfire's pocket of warmth and light. "The singing of it, the wondrous, evocative blending of words and melody, caused an immediate, commanding silence. It always does. *A-maz-ing grace, How sweet the sound. . . .*" Come let him refresh our memory on why and how we crumble crackers in soups and the consequences of contaminating chili with beans; a felony, argues Jerry. We'll explore the Guadalupe Mountains on horseback and travel the backroads of East Texas by car, searching for Mr. Colquitt's syrup mill. We'll revisit the original Texas topless rock 'n roll band, the Ladybirds, and partake in the organized social ritual of a hog killing. We'll get the skivvy on newspapers, the lowdown on hunkering, and the lore and legend of the lowly pecan. We'll learn how to say "ya'll." And why. We'll grumble with him over the dwindling number of real beer joints and the muddled lyrics of today's popular music: "Having not understood a song lyric since 1965, they all sound like 'Hokapeigtwubabysvcipkgosuprak.'" Jerry will explain the trend toward public cussing and why it's a step forward. And he'll examine the phenomenon of near-death experiences: "Skeptical by nature and certainly by training, I am suspicious of what cannot be proven. To me, a near-death experience rates beside such cultural mythologies as kidnappings by extraterrestrials and Congress balancing the budget." Despite his skepticism, his revelation wallops you like a game-winning grand slam in the bottom of the ninth. Likewise, he solves the mystery of the vanishing pulley bone and discloses the felonious story behind the famous statue at the entrance of Fort Worth's Will Rogers Auditorium/Coliseum complex. He even divulges the dirty little secrets behind the failure of the secession movement by the poorly conceived Republic of Texas. He'll introduce us again to the unsinkable Marguerite Oswald, the salty and self-styled "Mother of History," and he'll slash away a veneer of political correctness to define the West Texas woman. And, finally, he will tell us wistfully of his East Texas Brigadoon: "Somewhere in East Texas is my Brigadoon, a forested version of that magical Scottish town that appears just once each 100 years. Every year when fall arrives I think about it, where it is, and why I have never been able to find it again. I remember it and the day I spent there decades ago, as one of the most pleasant places and times of my life. Why can't I find it again?" With all my heart, I hope he has.

Mike Cochran
September 1999

Curmudgeon in Corduroy

The Best of

Jerry Flemmons' Texas

And Flights of Harlots Sing Thee To Thy Rest

Here's the lexicon of legendary symbols that defines Fort Worth's place in the epic path of Manifest Destiny: cowboys and longhorn steers, the mustang, Colt six-shooters, angels, stalwart soldiers, buffalo hunters, spurs and boots and big hats, the long rifle, ranches and ranchers. An indisputable master list of dramatic, artistic iconography affirming Fort Worth as a spiritual taproot of the American western experience.

Now, with the unveiled plans for Fort Worth's new performance hall for the symphony, ballet, opera, and other arts groups, we have conclusive—angels?—architectural testimony of the traditional brawny and virile character that—angels?—built Fort Worth into. . . .

Where in the hell did those angels come from?

Angels didn't build Fort Worth, didn't tame the frontier. John Wayne never rode with a posse of angels. Yet there they are: two forty-plus-foot-tall sculpted angels fronting our proposed block-sized downtown performing arts complex.

Fort Worth De Los Angeles? Frankly, I'm baffled, but so, apparently, is architect David Schwarz, who said of his angels, "I don't know where they came from. One day they weren't here. The next day they were."

Truth is, the miraculous appearance of angels was caused more by Schwarz's challenge to fill empty front wall space than immaculate conception, and what should be our Mount Rushmore on which to immortalize Fort Worth's heroic, manly past is instead an architectural vacancy for hanging feathered figures of shabby virtue and no recognizable gender.

We could have giant spurs, or blazing six-guns, or hook'em steer horns, or—for ethnicity's sake—two towering Joe T. Garcia's tacos, even noses-out profiles of the Sundance Kid and Butch Cassidy or, to establish a musical connection, Van Cliburn and Bob Wills. As a tribute to the Bass family's support, we could have bas-relief images of our earthly "angels," the understood expression for modern patrons of the arts. But no. . . . We get sleek and anonymous heraldic angels seemingly modeled from a pair of 1940s hood ornaments.

At the root of all this is the architectural style Schwarz chose. Beaux-arts revival, as it's called, is a kind of grab-bag approach that takes pieces of past classic forms and melds them into a miscellaneous whole—a Gothic cornice here, a Greek Revival truss there, a Doric fascia over a Queen Anne baluster, angels instead of tacos, that sort of thing. Beaux-arts was a building craze of nineteenth-century Europe, and angels were the ornamentation of choice, though not a critical success—"hollow idealism," to quote one reviewer of decorative angels. To simplify: 100 years ago, architectural angels were the Old Country equivalent of pink plastic flamingos on the front lawn.

But angels then enjoyed one of their periodic resurrections among the low masses, as they do right now with baby boomers and new-agers, many of whom believe in guardian angels as kind of celestial school-crossing guards for passing through the shadowy streets of modern life. The trouble with angels is that the Lord gave them free will, a big mistake, as transgressing angels began dropping from the heavens—a veritable cloudburst of sin-stained seraphim—almost as soon as God got the world started.

Our angels, architect Schwarz declared, are musical symbols, and there's some biblical precedence for that theory—in Revelations, trumpet-blowing angels announce the end of the world. But trumpeting angels, and those with harps and pan pipes, more are images of Renaissance artists like Botticelli and Caravaggio, who produced swan-winged, sweet-faced angelic creatures at play in the fields of man, ignoring traditional lore that angels are a hedonistic and carnal bunch. (One account noted that angels are "unquestionably susceptible to a friendship of the thighs," though other researchers question whether angels actually have "appliances for conjugation"—note how this entire angel research thing is fraught with carefully worded smut.)

So we have robed angels with protrusive trumpets from which to dangle holiday flags and pennants, two apparently androgynous cosmic cross-dressers at odds with historical fact that virtually all angels were male, and decidedly out of step with Fort Worth history and image.

Naturally, there were a few female angels. Gabriel is considered feminine because she sat on the left hand—the inferior southpaw position—of God. And there was Lilith, whose lascivious behavior got all mention of her deleted from modern Bibles. Lilith was Adam's original wife, but, to quote one scholar, was too "lively and wild." So Adam, who was the first man unable to deal with a strong woman, swapped Lilith for Eve. And Lilith went to hell as the Devil's favorite bride, thus becoming the earliest known fallen female angel. Her daughters were called the "Lilim" and the "Harlots of Hell" who. . . .

Wait a minute! Lilith, the matriarch of harlotry? And what were earthly prostitutes called? Fallen angels! I believe we're on to something here. Could this have been Schwarz's hidden agenda? He gives us angels as a subtle, perceptive salute to Fort Worth's once-grand shopping mall of sin, Hell's Half Acre, and the legion of fallen angels who labored there.

The Acre was a marvelous place in Fort Worth's western heritage. There were joints like the White Elephant, the Local Option, the Waco Tap, and the Headlight, which allowed cowboys to ride their horses up to the bar and drink from the saddle. The Two Minnies saloon had above its bar a glass-floored ceiling on which strolled nude girls—"nekked as a jaybird," to quote one witness, who threw back his head to take a drink, looked up, and couldn't swallow.

Women of the Two Minnies rented for $3 an hour, a moderate fee somewhat above the social scale of the two-bits-for-a-quickie girls and below the $10-a-night demimonde of the upscale sporting houses—one of which, operated by a madam named Lee Summers, was behind the El Paso Hotel on Houston and Fourth streets, very near our proposed performance hall, but that just may be coincidence. The battalion of women who serviced our men who won the West had wonderful names, and the Acre nurtured dozens of Nells and Belles, Lizzies and Tizzies, Frannies, Annies and Fannies—and finally, they are forgotten and anonymous no more.

We believe the two heraldic angels should have more

abundant bustlines, and for clarity's sake, symbolic names. We nominate a pair of popular girls of the period: Irish Kate will be the right angel, Big Birdie is the angel on the left. Around our frontier-born city are statuary pieces of cowboys and longhorns and horses. Now, thanks to architect Schwarz, we have angels. Again.

Autumn, We Hardly Knew Ye

Last Monday while I wasn't paying close attention—I took the morning off to settle the Bosnia problem—the 1997 Dog Days of Summer were declared officially closed, meaning, claims the dictionary, that finally this year's "hot and uncomfortable days" are done with, the heat and humidity are leaving, autumn is almost upon us.

A radio guy actually said: "Autumn is almost upon us." Surely he's newly arrived from some place Up There and just as certain serving his first sentence in Texas heat and still unable to pronounce "Mexia." He genuinely expects cooler days now that the calendar and mythology have called off the hot dogs of summer.

He will discover that Texas does not have autumn, which is a marketing concept of New England, a wholly owned subsidiary of Kodak. Instead of autumn, we have a spell of time called "fall" that occurs between the start of deer hunting and the first Christmas sale. Usually Thanksgiving, with its centuries of sacred gathered-family heritage, comes along somewhere in the middle of fall, though in short fall years when summer hangs on beyond all calendar rationality, the overheated Domino delivery cars arrive well after the kickoff and the blessing is delayed until halftime.

Because Texas is so large, fall has geographical implications. Down in the Rio Grande Valley, fall is known affectionately as "El Whew," and citizens celebrate by running through the streets yelling "Whew! Whew!" at one another because the heat index plunges into the low three figures. Sometimes people are so giddy with the arrival of fall that they commit folk dancing. At the same time, up in the Panhandle, in Amarillo and Dalhart, fall, most years, lasts completely through the lunch hour, and people miss it entirely if they linger over dessert.

The radio guy will learn that Texas, an over-achiever in all ways, doesn't limit itself to a skimpy four-season year. Beginning with after-Christmas white sales, the Texas seasons are: Intermittent Northers, Bluebonnets, Hay Fever, Tornado (alternately called "Hail"), Hot, Real Hot, Most Hot, My-Gawd-the-Heat, Football, and Fall. Now and then, we throw in a Drought season to break the monotony.

Texas summer heat is oppressively conscienceless as it rounds the calendar corner and bulldozes straight through the scheduled mid-September beginning of fall and leaps atop pitiable October, a festive month in autumn states like Vermont where Kodak forces all visitors to take photos of dewy-morning leaves turned brown and yellow and umber and crimson. Here leaves don't dew up. That's sweat.

Finally inertia and PTA Halloween carnivals bring summer's heat down to a tolerable level just about the time high school football teams begin their all-important district game schedules—powerhouses like the Trent Gorillas take on the Blackwell Hornets. The purest evidence of fall's arrival in Texas is Odessa's Mojo being tested against the Midland Lee Rebels, Stephenville battling Brownwood, the Kangaroos of Killeen vs. the 'Dogs of Copperas Cove. Fall's here when everywhere, all at once, people stand up and shout in unison: "On to state!" and there's a crisp, tangy aroma of concession stand Frito Pie in the air.

Frito Pie is our fall food and Texas' salute to Vermont's autumn because it contains all of New England's fall foliage tones—the brown of Fritos, the mahogany shades of good, rich chili, the white of finely chopped onion, the glossy yellow of shredded cheese—it's an opulent palette of nature's colors.

There's a large home (and school lunch) version of Frito Pie—an oven casserole—but it is best eaten at a Friday night high school football game concession stand, made by a PTA mama or one of the Spirit Club teenagers. Here's the recipe:

> You take a small bag of Fritos and lightly crush the chips. Slit the bag along one side with a sharp knife. Pour in hot chili equal to one-half the bulk of the broken Fritos, add a handful of finely chopped onion, top with a few fingers of shredded cheese. Mix well. Tradition and proper etiquette require that PTA Frito Pie be eaten with a plastic spoon.

If he's alert, that's what the radio guy will learn about autumn in Texas. He doesn't know much about Dog Days. Though the image of dogs panting under front porches in mid-August is a true cultural image of Texas, Dog Days have nothing to do with dogs. It's an astrological thing. Monday was the last day we could view the brightest summer star in the Canus [dog] Major constellation. It's called Sirius.

So, the heat hangs on, and on, and on. We're months away from Frito Pie season, but the Trent Gorillas already are warming up. On to state.

A Friend Falls
In the
Forest

Lance Rosier was an old man when he died. The irony in his death seems to be that his beloved Big Thicket as a continuous life force died before he did. Rosier, a squinty-eyed bantam-weight, did not drink, smoke, or dip snuff, nor did he drive or even own a car. He lived in Saratoga. At 120 pounds he was a huge man in everything but ambition. Rosier wanted only to walk within what remained of the Big Thicket.

There was precious little remaining of the Big Thicket. Oil and lumber companies, particularly lumber companies which own the land "clean down to China and clear up to the sky," as Lance said, are to blame along with real estate developers out for a quick buck and uncaring politicians. No one else.

The Big Thicket, as one writer believed, was a biological island of rare plant and animal life, a "giant wild garden being looted." A hundred years ago the Big Thicket covered three million acres. Today fewer than 300,000 acres remain and conservationists believe the existing forest disappears at the rate of fifty acres a day, about the area of six city blocks.

Originally, the Thicket covered eleven counties from Nacogdoches to Beaumont and from the Sabine to the Trinity rivers. Take a droplet of mercury and strike it with a hammer. The mercury separates and forms tinier, isolated beads. That is the Big Thicket today.

Quite probably no other place in the world resembles the original Big Thicket because it is where three distinct climatic zones live in harmony. For subtropic proof there are magnolia, palmetto palms, and more than twenty kinds of wild orchids. Yet mesquite and cactus—desert plants—are nearby. There is an abundance of plants characteristic to the Appalachian Mountains. The Thicket produces wild rhododendrons and azaleas, great banks of honeysuckle and verbena, spider lily, and wisteria. There are, in the world, five carnivorous plants—that is, plants that catch and eat insects. Four—the bog violet, sundew, bladderwort, and pitcher plant—are native to the Big Thicket.

Scientists speak of the Big Thicket as a "region of critical speciation." They mean that the climate, soil, and other botanical elements combined to create environmental change within plants. More than 100 different trees and plants grow in the Thicket. Something over 300 species of birds nest in the forests. The ivory-billed woodpecker was seen recently. Naturalists believed it had been extinct for three decades.

Big business, as usual, is blamed for the decline of the Big Thicket. Big business, as usual, deserves the blame. Loggers have ripped away most larger trees, especially hardwoods because more money can be made on pine. Bulldozed roads run in a straight line with no care to what may have lain in their paths. Oil pipelines were laid with no consideration for saltwater overflows. Land developers cut up the land, cut down trees, and sold five-acre ranchettes.

For more than forty years Lance Rosier watched his beloved Big Thicket disappear, fought against it, begged for its protection as a national park. By normal standards he was an uneducated man. As a self-taught naturalist, one of the best in the world, Lance knew each plant and its Latin name, knew each animal and its forest habits. Professors with Ph.D.s dangling from their names came to learn from the skinny-necked, plain-spoken old man. When Drs. Corey and Parks arrived in Saratoga researching their authoritative *Biological Survey of the East Texas Big Thicket*, Rosier had to locate and identify most of the plants for them. Other doctors from Venezuela, Norway, and Japan came to Rosier to learn. He was a sort of woodsy Aristotle who would teach what he knew to anyone.

What's left of the Big Thicket today is hard to find, and no one knows it as Lance did. He died of cancer. He was sixty-seven. The Big Thicket died of neglect and abuse. It was a million or so.

Putting the
Peas in
Prosperity

Time once again to explain to emigrants newly arrived from the United States why eating black-eyed peas is compulsory in Texas on New Year's Day. If it's not a state law, it should be.

Good luck—365 days' worth of happiness, prosperity, and well-being—is the simplest clinical rationale for eating black-eyed peas on the first day of the year. Don't eat them, and it'll be a rotten 1998 for you. This is proven fact. A couple of years ago, a guy I know—a scoffing newcomer from Up There—didn't eat black-eyed peas on New Year's Day. By February his wife had run off with a long-haul trucker, and his son had been outfitted with a navel ring. You can bet he planned on a black-eyed-pea meal to begin the next New Year. It just doesn't pay to defy science. Eat those peas.

How they're eaten is of no special concern—cold and straight from a can satisfies the luck factor—but black-eyed peas are a delicacy deserving an imaginative approach. Slow-cooked with hog jowls (or ham chunks, if your supermarket is short on jowls) and then spiced to taste with a vinegary Tabasco pepper sauce is one tradition-tested method. Peas and jalapeno slices is another. A third way could be "Texas caviar": well-drained peas mixed with oil, vinegar, bits of onion, garlic, and peppers. Marinate three days before eating.

However they're fixed, black-eyed peas should be the core dish of a New Year's Day meal, and cornbread is the finest kind of accompanying Texas comfort food but only if prepared correctly, which means yellow—not white—corn-meal with no sugar and just a smidgen of wheat flour, cooked in a hot cast-iron skillet.

Now we've got three subjects going on all at once here, but they're related through tradition and history, each necessary to the others. Folklore says black-eyed peas and good luck were linked after the Civil War, when hungry southerners were forced to eat cowpeas, formerly a cattle fodder quickly renamed black-eyed peas. More likely, good-luck foods on New Year's Day came in the package of beliefs brought by English and Scottish settlers—including "first step" (the first person entering the house in the new year should be a dark and handsome stranger, who brought good luck) and opening all windows and doors to allow a home's harmful spirits to leave.

However the tradition began, there's no question that cornbread was eaten with black-eyed peas. Corn, the most versatile of our vegetables, was the survival food that sustained settlement of America. Indians, of course, introduced corn to Pilgrims, and in appreciation we took their lands. Unlike wheat (from which white flour is made), corn grows almost anywhere, which is the reason cornmeal was available as the frontier food. Its uses seem endless.

It's boiled on the cob. Shelled fresh, it mixes easily into a stew-like hoppin' john or joined with beans and squash it's succotash. There's cornstarch. It pops. Cows and pigs grow fat on it. Cooked, hulls removed by lye, it's hominy, which when ground becomes grits. Fine sour-mash bourbon and an acceptable beer can be made from corn. There's fried cornbread; and, when thin, hoecakes (because they were literally cooked on hoes) and pancakes (best eaten with thick molasses, as pioneers did) and even waffles. I have seen a recipe for cornbread pizza dough.

It's the best dressing with turkey. It's fritters and spoonbread, a pudding, porridge, mush, and a basis for masa, from which tamales, tortillas, and chips are made. It's Indian fry bread, a perfect batter for catfish. Mixed with onions and other spices, it is a hush puppy, can be boiled into corn dodger balls, and baked with jalapeno peppers, onions, cheese, and even black-eyed peas—a recipe that won Athens' Black-Eyed Pea Cookoff one year.

Nothing of corn is wasted. Cattle eat its stalks. Rural boys smoked the tassels—cornsilk. Shucks wrap tamales for cooking or can be made into dolls, or used as mattress stuffing. (I once spent several nights in a Roman Catholic mission a day's mule-ride south of Creel in Mexico's western mountains, sleeping on a cornshuck mattress—very comfortable, but noisy.) The cobs were made into pipes and used as kindling to begin fires. They could be lighted at night as torches. A one-inch piece of corn cob was a serviceable fishing cork. And corn cobs, along with an old Sears, Roebuck catalog, were present in frontier outhouses everywhere (you've now learned the origin of the saying "rough as a cob").

So cornbread and black-eyed peas are in good-luck lock step as we march into the New Year. It's unlikely you've experienced the pleasures of gathering and shelling your own peas ("on the front porch of a hot summer evening with wisteria flowers perfuming the air and cicadas beginning their night song," as one Southern writer remembered). So buy them by the pound and cook as instructed.

For perfect cornbread, you'll need a nine-inch cast-iron skillet. It's possible to cook mediocre cornbread in those non-stick pans, but they do not create the necessary crisp undercrust. A century ago, cast-iron cookware was necessary because of wood-fire cooking. It could withstand high temperatures. A new bride usually brought inherited cast-iron pans and skillets to the marriage, and this was best because the cookware already had been cured. Curing a skillet takes time and patience; it requires baking in layers of grease and a black residue of many cooked meals.

Use a cornbread mix if you like (in Texas, yellow cornmeal is preferred), but an honest cornbread maker will go from scratch. There are two rules: use only a little white flour as a binder and sugar not at all. Only northern cooks flavor cornbread with sugar, producing something that southerners and Texans ridicule as "Yankee cake."

Heat the oven to the necessary temperature. Coat the skillet with bacon grease and heat it on a stovetop burner until it smokes heavily—then, and only then, pour in the cornbread batter; hear it sizzle, sealing the bottom crust. Stick it in the oven and wait.

One way to eat the meal is to split cornbread squares and spread them on a plate. Dribble on some pot liquor from the pan; then cover the bread with black-eyed peas. My favorite way is to alternate layers of peas, fresh tomatoes, and chopped white onions. Good eating.

Some say the good luck is multiplied if you give black-eyed peas and cornbread to friends and neighbors on New Year's Day. It can't hurt. Do all of this, and good fortune is assured. Don't eat black-eyed peas, and you'll be cursed. Remember that guy from two years ago, and his bad luck, his vow to eat black-eyed peas the next New Year's Day. The bad luck followed him throughout the year, and in late December he was in an automobile accident, injured just enough to put him in the hospital when the New Year rolled around. He missed the peas again. Sure enough, the bad luck continued. First thing that happened was the long-haul trucker brought his wife back. Eat those peas.

The Shadow
Of
Death

Charles Joseph Whitman lay in the shadow of his last afternoon.

At 1:50 p.m. the sun was moving away from the famed Tower at the University of Texas, and the west railing along the observation deck was spreading a pale gray shadow. Whitman lay there on his back, a carbine at his feet, in the northwest corner of the deck. The shadow cut diagonally across his body above the belt. His right leg was crooked away from the rifle. His foot rested on the railing's base.

Ten persons crouched along the narrow concrete walkway. Five were Austin policemen. Two were stretcher-bearers from an Austin ambulance service. Dr. Robert C. Stokes of the University Student Medical Center was there. Beside him was his nurse, a tight-lipped gray-haired woman. The tenth was a *Fort Worth Star-Telegram* reporter. A police lieutenant squatted beside Whitman, his knee in the sniper's blood.

"Is he dead?" he asked. "He looks dead."

"Just a minute," answered Dr. Stokes. The doctor was coatless; a stethoscope hung from his neck. He reached for Whitman's left hand and searched for a pulse. Another policeman came around the corner from the east side.

"Get down! Get down! They're still shooting," yelled the lieutenant. The officer dropped to the concrete.

"Who's shooting?" shouted the officer.

"Civilians. They've got rifles. Tell them to get somebody on the radio and stop 'em from shooting. Tell them it's all over," ordered the lieutenant.

"I don't want to get shot, now that it's over," shouted one of the ambulance men. He stretched out on the concrete.

"It is over," the lieutenant repeated to an officer beside him.

The officer nodded.

The tower observation deck, twenty-six stories above the campus, highlights Central Austin. On a clear day (and that Monday was a clear day) you can see the hills and lake country to the west of Texas' capital city.

"I heard Speed died [an Austin policeman shot earlier by Whitman]," the officer said aloud.

"Uh-huh," said another.

"Damn!" said the lieutenant, then added, "Well, is he dead? He's not breathing."

Dr. Stokes was feeling again for the pulse.

"They're bringing stretchers for the woman and the boy," said a voice out of sight along the wall.

"Damn," muttered the lieutenant. "What a mess."

The ten had seen the bodies of the boy and a woman a few minutes earlier when they came up in the tower elevator. It is a thirty-second ride up the elevator. No one liked what he found. Moments earlier, the officers, doctor and nurse, and stretcher carriers had left the small hallway. There was chaos on the first floor.

Officers shoved back the crowds of curious university students, most of whom had been hiding in buildings and behind trees and in stores along the school's west boundary, "the Drag" or Guadalupe Street.

One officer had a loudspeaker. Others shoved and pushed the students out of the tower's lower lobby. In front of the elevators, a man in khaki pants yelled to nobody in particular: "We need a priest. Get a priest here quick."

An officer gave the order. A minute or so later Father David O'Brien of the Catholic Student Center came down the hall, escorted by an officer.

"I was in the crowd," he said breathlessly. His black shirt was wet with August sweat.

"Go with the officers," he was told. He waited beside the elevators.

There was a series of clicks in the tower's elevator as it reached the lower, glassed-in observation deck. It clicked twice, then again, and the doors opened.

"My God," said a stretcher carrier. Father O'Brien let out his breath quickly.

There was the boy, on the floor in front of the elevator. The boy was young, in his teens. He was brown, possibly Latin, but blood covered his face. A gauze wadding was in his mouth. It, too, was blood-covered. He lay on his back, beneath the south window, his arms outstretched along his sides. The boy wore blue jeans and old shoes and his shirt was green, a light green that stood out against the white marble floor.

"God, here's another," shouted a voice. "It's a woman."

To reach the upper level of the observation deck, it is necessary to climb five steps. The narrow stairwell turns to the right.

She, too, lay on her back. Her left arm passed over her

forehead as though she were protecting herself. Her lips showed a thin line of blood. Her blood had filled the hall. It splashed as the party passed through it. Down the stairs, the elevator doors opened again and a second crowd came through. You could hear their murmuring voices as they passed the boy.

A black policeman came in from the outside observation catwalk. He had two rifles and a shotgun in his arms.

"Is that what he used?" someone asked.

"Part of it. The rest is with him, out there," said the policeman.

An empty shotgun shell lay in the doorway. About a dozen rifle casings were scattered in the marbled halls; above the door were bullet marks made by police firing from far below.

They found Whitman in the corner, with the shadow moving on him.

"Martinez [Austin police officer Ramiro Martinez] got him," said the lieutenant.

All crowded around the sniper. Someone reached under Whitman for his wallet. Whitman's driver's license was frayed at the edges, and the officer read aloud.

"Charles Joseph Whitman, Box 242. Is that Needville, or Weedville? I can't read it," asked the officer.

"How old was he?" some one asked.

"Uh, twenty-four . . . no . . . twenty-five."

"That's got to be Needville," the lieutenant decided. "Was he a student here?"

No one answered.

They waited there in the sun and the shadow and slight breeze. Ten minutes passed.

"He's dead," said Dr. Stokes finally. "We'd better wait before we move him though."

The crowd moved back toward the door, crouching below the railing. An officer hit a steel rifle casing with his hand as he moved. It skittered along the concrete, dropped through a water drain, and fell the twenty-six stories.

By the elevator, another pair of stretcher carriers was waiting with the woman's body. A man, slightly built, gray-haired, his eyes on the floor, stood beside them. He carried a pair of women's white high-heeled shoes. They were bloody. He also held a white purse.

"That's his wife," someone whispered.

He was asked his name.

"I don't believe I can say anything now. That's my wife there. I don't believe I can talk," he answered. His eyes stayed on the floor.

The man moved into the elevator with his wife's body. Inside, he stared at the ceiling.

[Police later identified the woman as Edna Townsley, the receptionist in the tower.]

Twenty minutes later, a stretcher came for the body of Charles Joseph Whitman. The ambulance man looked at Whitman for a long time. The sniper's blond hair, matted against a once-green sweatband about his head, was dark, almost black from the blood. The green fatigues, worn over a pair of jeans, and the ammunition belt he wore when shot were beside the body.

"I can't believe it," said one of the men.

"Me neither," answered the other.

They lifted Whitman from the concrete and placed him on the stretcher.

He was in the sun. The shadow was behind.

Of Dimple
And Dixie
And Dump

The other day I was searching for knowledge and came across an old book I hadn't read in years and remembered all over again that Waxahachie is a town nobody can spell and few pronounce correctly. There's a kind of avant-garde fame in such, and Waxahachie joins Mexia, Refugio, and San Jacinto in Texas name places that mostly are always mispronounced. Moreover, Waxahachie's name—which is Indian—carries the burden of a socially awkward definition. The name means . . . well, to be polite . . . cow chip (correctly, the name is slightly more colorful). A few historians of the chamber-of-commerce variety disagree, but Indians who know the language claim otherwise.

So that's that, and the proof is in *Place Names in Northeast Texas,* in which Dr. Fred Tarpley, then at Texas A&M/Commerce, had students chase down place name meanings. It's Dr. Tarpley we need to thank for knowing the smallish community of Mutt and Jeff in Wood County came because the hamlet's two leading merchants resembled those cartoon characters.

How we name places requires rich imagination and often a sense of humor. Frognot was named because residents killed all the frogs. Scratch Eye in Harrison County was coined because low tree branches around the town caused citizens to fear for their eyes. Grand Prairie became Grand Prairie because, tradition says, a woman traveler exclaimed, "My, what a grand prairie!" Ambia in Harrison County was named by a local justice of the peace to describe the amber jets of tobacco juice spat by its loafers around the general store. Karnack, birthplace of Lady Bird Johnson, was discovered by a local intellectual to be exactly the same distance from Caddo Lake as ancient Karnack in Egypt was from the Nile River.

Within the twenty-six East Texas counties covered in the old book, you literally could travel the world, moving from Paris to Malta, Macedonia, St. Helena, Scyene, Klondike, Dixie, Detroit, and Warsaw. Even "Warsaw" is not what it seems, not named for the Polish city but for the sound of Indians trying to pronounce the English word, "water."

Natural site names had the same eccentric beginning, such as the small creek that runs behind a cemetery at Leonard. Boney Creek, it was named. There's also Boardinghouse Creek, Cowhorn Creek, Swamppoodle Creek (named for a mud puddle, not a poodle dog; spelling was not always exactly precise), Greasy Creek, Middle Lilly Creek, Crooked Branch, Pigeon Roost Creek, and Doctors Creek. Ghost Creek, Buggy Whip Creek, Calaboose Branch, Carcass Hole, Cherry Boggy, Yellow Steer Slough, and possibly the finest name of all: No Name Creek.

Names reveal a religious nature in early settlers, at the communities of Bethlehem, Antioch, Hepsibah, Gethsemane, Smyrna, Old Egypt, Galilee, and Burning Bush.

And of course you've already heard of Fink and Bug Tussle. Texas stopped erecting town signs at Bug Tussle because souvenir hunters stole them.

There are—or were—Free Oneness, Hoot Index, Faker Switch, Hopeful (and conversely, Little Hope), Climax, Free Grass, Squeeze Penny School, Ticky Valley, Zip City (named by a woman who sat on her front porch and watched cars zip by), Old Granny's Neck, Three P, Peatown, Five Notch, Shoe String (because that's what local oil wildcatters operated on), Uncertain, Crush, Mud Dig, Grasshopper, Tinrag (the Garnit family name spelled backward), Jiba, Poetry, Peeltown, Pinhook, Frog Hop, Dimple, Shadowland, and Squash Hollow.

Some names came in nonsensical ways. Hurricane was named because a tornado struck there. Dump became Dump because a citizen exclaimed, "I don't care what we call this dump as long as we get a post office!" Orangeville was named because some newly arrived Yankees believed bois d'arc fruit were oranges. Gourd-Neck-or-Lick-Skillet became a settlement's name because no majority decision could be made about either so the village became both.

Can't-Cha-Get-Over Creek flooded often. Direct was named because an early revivalist told citizens they were going "straight to hell." Fulp is a family name. Little Flock explained the plight of a church with a meager attendance. Ragtown was populated by tidy folks who washed their clothes until they became tattered and torn. Wamba was a popular coffee brand, and Rugby was the maker of a kind of bicycle. Hog Eye resulted from the sharp look of a local pig thief. Most lyrical and certainly the most poetic of all northeast Texas place names is Sherry Prairie Cemetery, named for the Sherry family.

A lesson in place naming can be learned from Curtis Jernigan. Once he followed a deer into a dense thicket and became lost. After three days he heard a rifle shot and ran toward the sound. The man who fired the rifle, Jernigan discovered, was his worst enemy. So, placing pride before rescue, Jernigan ran back into the thicket and became lost again.

That's how Jernigan Thicket in Delta County was named.

Dawn

Comes

Sunny Side Up

The salvation of an early morning riser in West Texas is a somber truck stop cafe beside the interstate. Sleepy waitresses and soggy eggs. Silent coffee-drinkers and sagging booth seats in a wayside world sustained by the promise of a new day. A Formican oasis of chrome-legged stools and a diffident tranquility disturbed only by voices of truck stop waitresses, who yell their orders.

Two eggs, please, scrambled well done, with sausage and biscuits.

"SCRAMBLE TWO HARD, PATTIES AND BISCUITS! Coffee, hon?"

A vocal breakfast chorus, these sunny-side-up a cappella Annies, shrill enough to crack the dawn.

It is a myth, of course, about truck drivers and good cooking. They don't care much about first-rate food. Their restaurant choice is made by acreage allowance, space to park their monster rigs. Or discount diesel, a nickel off a gallon. Food in interstate truck stops is incidental and reasonably priced. Truckers like bulk, not quality. Large portions, quickly served, and basic. Every dish is a meatloaf special. The menu is all meat and potatoes, nothing fancy or strangely named—hamburger steak is Hamburger Steak, never *100 All-Beef, Freshly-Ground and Seasoned Chuck in Our Special Secret Sauce*. There are no secrets in truck stop cafes.

At 5:00 A.M. of a foggy morning in West Texas, an interstate truck stop is the entire cosmos. Only it is awake to serve. On the road, fog covers the desert and rises, steamlike, from ditch water. Dark bulks in pastures are cows or sheep or squatty cedar trees or creosote bushes, all unmoving and cold in the chilled wet air. The interstate merely shows up out of the fog, a flat, gray concrete ribbon carrying 18-wheelers and ubiquitous ranch pickups into the pasture-sized parking lot. There are cattle trucks and refrigerated trucks and long-haul moving trucks packed with family possessions, trucks full of wholesale foodstuffs, trucks hauling K-Mart Blue Light Specials, beer-bearing trucks, and trucks headed west with loads of farm produce. The pickups are left to fend for themselves amid the 18-wheelers, pebbles among boulders, laden with hay bales and farm tools, coiled ropes, rolls of barbed wire, colicky calves, here and there old worn saddles—the detritus of hard-scrabble living on the plains.

On damp foggy mornings cafe windows mist over, hiding the coffee-drinkers, who are mostly cowmen waiting for sale barns to open up somewhere down the road. Truckers are the eaters. They've worked up an appetite driving through the night fog. And as they order, the waitresses announce their food like auctioneers taking bids:

"STEAK AND TWO OVER EASY! PAIR 'EM, UP AND SUNNY, SIDE OF HAM! MORE COFFEE OVER HERE! A STACK AND LINK!"

All of this is yelled to the cook. Not chef, never a chef. He stands, framed through the order window, guarding his grill. For no obvious reason, all truck stop cooks have hairy arms—many of them with faded tattoos—and wear yesterday's whiskers. Their shirt sleeves are rolled elbow high, not neatly turned but rolled and pushed up, and their hands move about the grill with startling speed, like shell game con men hiding the peanut.

Within the foggy-windowed room of an interstate cafe, the coffee-drinkers are copies of one another, all assembled in a common pre-dawn position. A drinker hunches his shoulders, places each elbow on the table and holds, with both hands, the motionless cup, his holy grail of cheap off-white industrial china. He stares at something over the mug's edge and drinks when he remembers what he is there for. His hat, whether basic western or modified cowman, is never removed. He is a stoic thinker, drinking coffee only to steam his thought processes. All of this is performed to an accompanying clatter of dishes and silverware, murmurs of low words, scuffling and shuffling of feet, and theme music from a neon-bright jukebox.

Trucker songs, maybe an old Dave Dudley ode of diesel despair. Pavement psalms. There are guitars chording anthems of agony and the brisk pizzicato fiddle runs between verses and going-home choruses. Songs old and sad, new and forlorn. A Mother Maybelle Carter doing "Wildwood Flower" or Hank Snow singing "Ninety Miles an Hour" in the key of nasal B-flat, interrupted now and then by a Clint Black electrified epistle or a Tanya Tucker mean-man sermon or a sanguine homily from one or more Judds, ol' Willie wailing for another hopeful dawn.

Dawn erases the mood and setting. The fog burns away,

and the truckers take to the interstate again. The pickup riders leave, heading for the cow barns. The parking lot empties. And the waitresses no longer yell orders but drink their own cups of coffee within a miasma of cigarette smoke, waiting for the next pack of Mack rigs to come for five cents off a gallon of diesel and the meatloaf special at a steamy interstate truck stop cafe in far, far West Texas.

Out of the Frying Pan and
Into the Internet—
Fry, Fry Again

The point about this is the sorry state we've let chicken-fried steak get in out there in America while we've been dealing with Bosnia, the silly Joe Camel crusade, and how to get those people from Arkansas out of the White House before they begin holding garage sales.

It's a known fact that Texas dishes don't travel well beyond our borders—outsiders seem unable to grasp the subtleties of a Tuesday Special Tex-Mex enchilada plate or mesquite-fired beef BBQ or the need for chow-chow on freshly cooked black-eyed peas, certainly not the ethical maintenance of that most endearing and enduring Lucullan feast, the chicken-fried-steak meal.

I have been tracking Texas foods in cyberspace, and the situation's no better there, either, specifically at the Internet Chef website (www.ichef.com) where a "Chicken [no hyphen] Fried Round Steak" recipe is listed. First of all, aside from the truant hyphen, there's a blatant redundancy. A proper chicken-fried steak always is tenderized round steak, a cheap and tough piece of beef because that's all early rural Texans—the inventors of chicken-fried steak—could afford.

For identification purposes, "round" steak, a knowledgeable Texas cook once told me, is "the part the cow lays down on." For non-animal-husbandry majors, cows lie on their right sides, so the best round-steak source for a proper chicken-fried steak is sliced from the right rear side of a cow, behind the stomach but short of the tail, back by the hips, perpendicular to the udders. You could talk it over with your meat-counter person, who once was called a butcher before shrink-wrapped pre-packaging. But I digress.

The worst offense of the Internet Chef's recipe is its recommended use of cracker crumbs as batter. Cracker batter? That suggests the chef filched the recipe from the back of a box of Shake 'n Bake. Immediately I e-mailed the chef to explain that finely milled flour is the honest foundation for good batter, that saltines in Texas are crumbled only into chili, and please replace the hyphen. I haven't heard back yet, but sound advice is not often heeded these days.

At another internet site, I read of a misplaced Texan driving across Montana, where he discovered "to my horror, that some restaurants up there serve a chicken-fried steak ON TOP OF THE GRAVY!!" He went on: "The steak is sort of plopped down in a puddle. Beyond the inconceivable aesthetics of such a scene, one is stymied as to how to EAT it!! All the lifelong techniques of gravy-to-meat allotment are voided." He suggested that we "establish a geographical line west and/or north of which one should be aware of this danger." A chicken-fried steak DEW (distant early warning) line seems impractical and probably ineffectual, because outsiders appear insensitive to our culture. You only have to look at what they've done to BBQ.

BBQ is beef. Texans know that. We invented it. But cross the Louisiana state line and BBQ becomes, mostly, pork and other pig parts. Long ago, writer Griffin Smith explained in *The Atlantic* what BBQ is not. He lectured: "It is not shredded pork . . . as North Carolinians sell in gold-fish cartons." The situation in North Carolina may be that—and this is a statistical fact—it has more pigs than people and pork is barbecued exclusively as a kind of population control program. Pork BBQ is mushy, not firm and tasty like real beef BBQ. I tasted pork BBQ once in Memphis and had to wash out my mouth with half a bottle of Dr Pepper.

One problem with exporting Texas dishes along the eastern seaboard is that we've lost our White House connection. LBJ brought in the late, legendary Walter Jetton's Texas BBQ for parties in the Rose Garden, and Ladybird was known to have taught chicken-fried-steak secrets to White House chefs. Even George Bush served Texas BBQ and chicken-fried steak. But the current occupant is oriented toward Golden Arches' coupon specials, and McDonald's, unlike Dairy Queen, does not offer a chicken-fried steak (though its menu does feature a decent line of synthetic hamburgers).

It's enough to know that once I passed a Hot Springs BBQ joint that advertised "Barbecued Baloney." My lord! That goes a long way in explaining our current Washington crisis. But I have further digressed.

Unless we set up a string of Texas cooking schools across America or regularly send out chicken-fried-steak missionaries, like the Mormons do, this problem isn't going away. It's best just to eat it at home or in a local cafe—800,000 chicken-fried steaks are served daily, estimates the Texas Restaurant Association. What the TRA does not say is how many of those chicken-fried steaks were—and this is a growing plague—pre-formed and flash-frozen. Before ordering, it's always best to ask, "This is not one of those frozen things, is it?"

And today most likely even good chicken-fried steak will be deep-fried. Few Texas restaurants take the effort and time to cook chicken-fried steak the traditional way, which is in a large cast-iron skillet with very little oil. Afterwards, the milk-based gravy is made right in the pan so it has little bitty flecks of batter for texture and flavoring. That's the way you cook it at home.

Meanwhile, beyond our borders, out on the road, the chicken-fried steak horror stories keep coming in. In Oregon, for example, a Texas businessman discovered "Real Texas Chicken-Fried Steak" on a small-town restaurant menu and quickly ordered it.

"Yes, sir," said the young waiter, adding expectantly, "and how would you like that cooked?"

Doylene Bradshaw of Anson, Texas, has been cooking chicken-fried steak since the early 1950s. For more than thirty years she cooked it every day for lunch for her husband, three daughters, friends, and assorted in-laws. It is recommended that one be generous with portions, as Doylene's Chicken-Fried Steak goes fast.

Doylene's Chicken-Fried Steak

- Get some round steak, a pound or so.
- Beat vigorously with edge of plate to tenderize.
- Doylene says: "Don't dip in batter or milk. Just rinse in cold water and dust it in flour. Gold Medal All Purpose is good." Doylene says you don't want the breading to overpower the taste of the meat.

• Put just enough grease in to cover the bottom of skillet. She says: "Have to use Crisco, not the oil but the kind in a can."

• You want the fire going pretty good because you don't want to cook it slow, and you sure don't want it overcooked. Start it on high so it really sizzles, and then cut it to medium so it doesn't burn.

• Put steak in skillet and brown on one side and then turn it. That's when you salt it. Can do pepper if you want. Cook until as brown as you want.

Doylene's Gravy

Drain off most of the grease. Of course you like to keep that good old breading that fell off the steak. Should be about three tablespoons of grease left. Add a tablespoon of flour and one-third cup of water and make a paste. Keep adding milk until you get the right consistency. ("This doesn't make a lot of gravy," says one of Doylene's daughters, "but Doylene doesn't like a lot of gravy.") Gravy does not go on steak but is served on side for white bread. Some people like to tear their bread in little pieces and cover with gravy. It's a West Texas thing.

Doylene believes chicken-fried steak is always served with fried potatoes.

A Boy's Life,
before
Litigation

I'm thinking about getting into the child-protection racket. Currently, this is a flourishing business, and I'm keen to collect a salary for thinking up ways to save children from themselves and us and any perceived risk, however far-fetched, in daily life.

The way I understand the profession is that whatever anybody thinks is a good idea for society, I'm paid to stand up and yell, "Hey, wait a minute, think of the children." Most of the good child safety laws have been thought of, but deep within my boyhood lies a rich vein of possible playtime hazards that require only risk assessment and speedy legislation to ensure fail-safe lives for the few remaining children with freedom to play spontaneously and creatively (basically, I'm speaking only of little boys, who are born with adventuresome genes).

They could, to begin with, take up dirt fights, specifically with dirt clods. One natural law is that, given the opportunity, little boys will throw things, and, free to choose, they will throw those things at one other. "Chunk," as the practice once was known. In hot summertime, Texas dirt shrivels and cracks. It's possible to prize up a hand-size clod of dirt and chunk it a fair distance. If a few of us were standing around in August, idly chunking dirt clods, invariably someone would begin a dirt-clod war, with assorted points granted for strikes above and below the beltline. Taking a direct hit in the back was akin to dying on the battlefield. Dirt clods hurt, but the rule was you couldn't ever admit it.

Rubber-gun fights were slightly less bloody than dirt-clod wars. These guns were made from old inner tubes and scrap lumber. First, using your mother's best scissors, you cut many one-inch strips from the tube—they looked like giant rubber bands. A two- to three-foot length of 1x4 lumber, cut to resemble a crude rifle, was the gun. A clothespin was attached to the rear of the gun. A tube ring was hooked over the front end of the gun and stretched back to the clothespin, which held a fold of the tube. All you did was aim, fire by pressing the clothespin, and the rubber band snapped away like a howitzer. Really inventive rubber gunsmiths took longer 1x4s, cut half a dozen notches along the rear, hooked the bands into the notches, and made machine guns. These were fired by laying a string along the notch line and lifting it from the back—the bands would zing off singularly or, with a full pull, fire like a scattergun. Heavy casualties were assured. Rubber-gun fights were stealth operations, best fought along whole blocks, from house to house, attempting to catch the enemy not looking. A well-placed rubber gun shot stung.

It was only a small step from rubber guns to BB-gun fights, the only battle game we played with rules. Actually, one rule: no fair shooting above the shoulders. BB-gun fights required sneakiness, but you could fire from a greater distance with more accuracy. Generally, BB fights followed a western movie plot line, and anyone fatally wounded was allowed to perform a theatrical death. BBs really stung the skin, and usually left a red mark. No one could claim he wasn't hit.

A decent rubber-band gun could be fashioned from a plain clothespin. The making of one is far too complicated to go into here (you have to dismantle the thing, reverse one wood piece, cut an extra notch . . . well, it goes on). With a clothespin gun you could fire grains of corn or small pea gravel with fair accuracy. We used them only for close combat. Even closer, we shot kitchen matches at one another with the clothespin guns. The matches came out flaming. Or you could devise a very clever dart from a match, a sewing needle and two tiny strips of newspaper for a tail. Usually we threw only at feet, but it was a dangerous game because few of us wore shoes on hot summer days.

Fortunately, we've disarmed all citizens of fireworks, and no small boys will ever again be endangered by shooting off Roman candles or bottle rockets. Before fireworks became a spectator sport, we had our very best wars with firecrackers. A favored location was a small creek, one team on each bank, dug in behind fallen trees used as forts. You formed a mud-ball bomb around a firecracker, lit it, and chunked it toward the enemy, hoping it would explode all over somebody. Only the bravest would mud over a huge cherry bomb, hold it, and hold it as the fuse burned, then at the last moment fling it over the creek to produce an airburst, which slung stinging mud-pellet shrapnel everywhere.

We would fire Roman candle balls back and forth and only now and then try a horizontal bottle rocket shot, which was a tricky maneuver at best. Everyone went home powder-burnt and mud-speckled, and tired from what we called play, which those who study such matters know as a kid's socialization process.

You'll notice that none of these games required adult supervision or planning, uniforms or, afterwards, award ceremonies in which every participant got a trophy so no one's self-esteem would suffer. We crushed each other's self-esteem when we could and took no prisoners. Scores and winning mattered.

Almost no children experience free play anymore; we've organized play into regimen, and almost legislated away childhood in all forms. For the few adventuresome boys who do still run free in the sunshine, I would suggest that chunking dirt clods or having rubber-gun fights are not unhealthy ways to use up an afternoon. Or they could try this: on a day when no one's around to play with, take a towel, tie it around your neck as a cape, climb up on the roof edge, say the magic word, "Shazam!" raise your arms and fly off into . . . Better wear your helmet with this one. The landing's a little rough, as I recall.

Have
Rubber Gun,
Will Travel

"Amen to clod fights. [I've wondered] if clod fights took place all over the country or only in the Saginaw area. A well-placed clod near the ear could be pretty painful as could a mud-packed firecracker with a fast fuse that went off just as you had drawn it back to a few inches from your ear, ready to let it go. I can still feel it sixty years later."

—*Bill Sloan*

"I am sixty years old. I was in my early teens in Ennis. That is where my buddies and I made our rubber guns, single shot and multi-shot, and made war on each other. We did stupid things, dumb things and childish things. We made mistakes and we learned. It was a 'real world' maturing process. I feel sorry for most of the children of today because they are growing up in a sanitized environment."

—*Basil G. Garrett*

"You captured a better time, I believe, when you remembered the weapons most of us made as little boys, precious moments just after mothers and before girls. Do you remember nature's own weapon, the good ol' sticker burr? Cast with just the right amount of spin and velocity it would sink a five-headed burr fairly deep into the skin of someone's back. Ahhh, what good times those were.

"My first thought was that times have changed, but then I remembered the fort that my six-year-old has built in our backyard: black plastic and wood, a bungee cord, a stolen scrap of carpet and an American flag. The weapons he will make are not too far behind, I can tell. And I realize, too, that the only thing that has changed is me."

—*David Van Meter*

"When I was growing up on Avenue J in Poly the Lawsons in the next block had a slew of kids, so it was everybody else against the Lawson Gang (not a bad word then). On reflection, the thing that impresses me now is how much we learned that was already known and how much the basics have not changed.

"Technology transfer, for example. Was the rubber machine gun invented everywhere at the same time, or did it travel with the new kid who moved into the block?

"One of the Lawsons was a girl who 'rode' with them, carried the ammo and did a little spying. A moll. Our side never had one.

"Prisoner exchange. We were doing this at ten years old.

"Arms limitations. When our side got an old round porch post, cut it into two-foot lengths, nailed on notched wood and made Gatling guns, the Lawsons insisted on a fair share of the post or no Gatling guns on our side.

"Not related was a technology event in our young lives. My best buddy and I found a rocket fuel recipe in a magazine. We got the ingredients at Cloud's Pharmacy on Vaughn Boulevard. We mixed it up, stuffed it into a piece of pipe with a cap on one end, laid it on his front porch swing and lit it.

"The results were a large black circle on the wall behind the swing, a small hole in the house across the street, a larger hole in their sofa, and a charred spot on their rug under our pipe.

"All these boys were the ones who, a few years later, marched off to save our country and the world. You have made me think that all the stalking weapons, play and inventiveness just might have helped them a little. Some of them came back and got into the defense business. They did the same things they did when they were kids. The only difference was that they got paid for it.

"One question for you: where do you think the age cutoff point is for readers who understand 'inner tube' and clothespin?

"Also I have forgotten how to make a clothespin gun. Can you help?"

—Joe Jopling

Mr. Jopling, I suspect you have to be at least thirty to know about inner tubes and wooden clothespins, even older to have seen and used a backyard clothesline (clothes dried by sun and wind smell fresher). As for the clothespin gun, if I can find wooden clothespins and figure it out again, detailed instructions, with an illustration, should be attached to this. If not, it means the editor is one of our too-young smart alecks who would ask where to insert the batteries in rubber guns and has wasted the space on silly written nonsense like world peace.

The following is taken from instructions in an excellent book, *Texas Toys and Games* (edited by Francis Edward Abernethy, UNT Press, 1997, $16.90, paper).

How to Make a Clothespin Gun

1. Get one wooden clothespin.
2. Take the clothespin apart by removing the metal spring. Now you have two wooden sticks with curved indentations.
3. Use a sharp knife to convert one of the indentations into a notch, "so that the forward side of the notch is perpendicular to the straight back of the wooden clip."
4. Use tape or string to "tightly bind the handle ends of the clips together so that the jaws of the clothespin remain open. The taped end is the butt end of the gun; the open end is the barrel."
5. "Position the spring on the bottom of the gun with the lower L in its original slot and the upper L resting on the inside of the lower jaw."
6. "The spring now becomes the trigger. Cock the gun by forcing the inside L back into the new-cut notch."

That's it: a clothespin gun. Cocking it is hard, though, as the book advises, "an extra clothespin clip makes a good cocking stick."

To load, push the "bullet" back against the firing pin. Find a target, aim and pull the trigger. And there you are. BBs and pea gravel shoot better if a groove is carved down the center of both wooden halves to make a kind of barrel. As for matches, shove the match head against the firing pin. The pin should strike and light the match, but today's safety matches have been made so safe they hardly light on anything.

On the Square
It's Half Past
Then

Now and then on warm spring evenings, I stroll a block to the town square just to hear the courthouse clock strike the hour. The bell's cadenced tolling, crisp and sonorous, has a kind of incisive authority to it, a comfortable durability, one of the few modern sounds unchanged in a century or more.

The clanging bells of railroad steam engines and fire engines, the lonesome horns of trains and steamboats, a factory noon whistle—all disappeared into the electronic cacophony of the twentieth century. But the pealing bell of a courthouse clock remains as an audible bridge to the past and a welcoming call to the small-town square. Squares and courthouses, many of them Victorian and of grandiloquent style, are the focal points of small towns, architectural traditions older than Texas because the Spanish brought the designs to the New World. In Spain, the centerpiece often was the church; here it is the county courthouse. Both places where the community did its public business, both surrounded by the symmetry of shops for trade goods and services.

This 1891 courthouse in Granbury, a small lakeside town in North Central Texas, I know well. Its square, which seems frozen in the 1920s, is on the National Register of Historic Places. The soaring tower of the white stone courthouse rises above the square like a castle spire and can be seen from almost anywhere in town.

All across the state, courthouses and squares are the same, yet different, personalized to their landscape and need and time. Just south, in Glen Rose, the courthouse is smaller but I can drink sulphury mineral water from a fountain in front, a legacy from the days when the town was a health spa. West, Stephenville's white, red-trimmed courthouse is noted for the statue of a cow on its lawn, and, as a pre-television child, I remember crowding into the square on state election nights to watch returns posted on a giant chalkboard.

Farther west, Ballinger's square is graced with a heroic-sized bronze statue of a cowboy and horse, symbolic of the area's ranching history. The Fleming Oak shades Comanche's courthouse lawn. In 1854, a young Martin Fleming hid from Indians behind its thick trunk. Decades later, the square was being prepared for paving, and the tree was to be cut down. A then-elderly Martin Fleming appeared with his rifle and defended the tree, as it once protected him. Displayed nearby is Comanche's first courthouse, built of logs in 1856.

Most first courthouses in Texas were built with logs (the current century-old Granbury courthouse is the sixth on the same site), but the mid-square positioning and use have never changed. The practical and determinedly democratic Greeks are credited with designing a municipal square surrounding a central government building. In Texas, distance from state government made the county courthouse essential for community business—a center for property deeds, trials both criminal and civil, marriages, registering of births and deaths, even public hangings. The enclosing square, early on, had a fort-like protective eminence, but gradually, as life outside was less threatening, squares became gathering places.

When Texas was mostly rural, the county courthouse square was a destination, especially on Saturdays when farming and ranching families came to town for supplies and visiting. When my family came in, all that our lives needed was around the square—a feed store for cattle grain and seeds, a grocery store for large bags of flour and cornmeal (the colorful cloth sacks were turned into necessary items like curtains and underwear), new shoes if school was beginning. We could have our pictures taken, a prescription filled, be fitted for new glasses.

I always got a quarter from the egg and butter money, and it bought a movie ticket, a fountain Coke from the drugstore, and afterwards, a hamburger and a used comic book. Life was full and rewarding. Progress has caused highway bypasses of many towns, and squares, such as Granbury's, now often turn to antique shops and cafes to entice customers.

Not all of Texas' courthouses are grand and old and historic. Some are block-shaped and utilitarian with neither bell tower nor stone ornamentation. Zapata's courthouse was built in 1953, as was the town; its old plaza and 1901 courthouse beside the Rio Grande today are under waters of Falcon Lake. Others have been foolishly remodeled into plainness.

More than seventy Texas courthouses—most on the

National Historic Register—remain with bell towers and clocks, cupolas and turrets, all the architectural ostentation of the last century. You have only to wander across the squares of Hillsboro or Waxahachie or Sulphur Springs, in the shadows of their soaring courthouses, to feel the past. Or, in East Texas, go to the huge red castle-like courthouse in Center where, on a sunny Saturday afternoon, old men still play dominoes on makeshift tables, large magnolias are in bloom, and children run across the lawn—a scene hardly changed in a hundred years.

And the bell of Granbury's clock resounds as it has for more than a century. It is a Seth Thomas Clock, number 16, with a four-sided face, and it works as it always has. It must be hand-wound every eight days by a volunteer who walks the steep interior stairs and climbs a final ladder to perform a civic duty that pays no salary, only the satisfaction of assuring the town that their bell always rings the hour.

John Donne's eternal counsel of whom the bell tolls for is correct. It tolls for thee and me, especially on a warm spring evening in a small Texas town.

The Way the Cracker Crumbles

Time again to reaffirm our Texas heritage of crumbling crackers for thin, watery soups such as vichyssoise (which restaurants, always looking to save a penny, insist on serving cold), clam chowder, and, especially, our official state dish of chili. Crumbling crackers, and sometimes cornbread, into foods like chili and stew is a timeworn Texas tradition. Crumbling crackers is our hard fought-for right.

Children, I feel sure, are not being trained in the art of cracker-crumbling because I see too many people not crumbling and all of them can't be newly arrived outsiders who are unaware of the crumbling tradition. This is disturbing, distressing. I saw an example of it the other day. A young lady was eating soup of some sort. She was dainty enough about it, but she actually—and here the trouble sits—ate her crackers one bite at a time. No crumbling at all. Sip of soup, pause, a nibble of crackers. The woman seemed respectable but obviously lacked a proper education in correct cracker styles. Or perhaps she was one of those etiquette rebels who's unconcerned about public manners. Some people don't care how they act in a restaurant. Assuming she was ignorant of The Cracker Rule, I'm sorry now I did not bring it to her attention. She would have appreciated the lesson, I'm sure. I do not know how widespread this vulgar, lowborn trend toward not crumbling has become (perhaps the backward young woman was an isolated case) but should it continue I think we can conclude that civilized dining is at an end as the millennium crashes down around us.

This is The Cracker Rule:

Crackers served with liquid food—whether oyster stew, chicken noodle soup, or chili—are to be crumbled. You will note that this simple yet eloquent statement is unequivocal. It does not qualify the mandate by suggesting that you crumble only if no one is looking. It commands one to crumble crackers. Period. It is gauche to do otherwise. (As a sidelight, Fritos make an excellent substitute to crumble in chili, as do oyster crackers in oyster soups.) How the cracker crumbles isn't important, and an individual may use whatever style he or she chooses. The basic rule, after all, simply is to crumble.

Personally, I favor the Nip Style. It's an easily learned skill. Hold the cracker gently between the thumb and forefinger and with the other thumb and forefinger slowly nip off pieces of the cracker. There are several reasons for my choice of the Nip Style. First, it is a quiet, genteel modus operandi: you don't disturb diners near you. Second, it causes the least amount of crumbs.

I have no strong disagreement with those who practice the Complete Hand Crusher and Brusher Method and, in fact, believe it displays a certain enthusiasm for eating and lends itself to gustatory showmanship, always a treat in restaurants that presume too much solemn decorum. The Complete Hand Crusher and Brusher Method advocates feel their way is best, and I will not argue. To each his own crumble, I say. A diner who hand crushes places the crackers in the center of the palm and swiftly, firmly, and decisively makes a hard fist. The cracker is powdered. His next move is to brush both hands together vigorously, eliminating the clinging crumbs. Critics have pointed out that the Hand Crusher practitioner produces much noise and far more crumbs than necessary. Too, spirited brushing tends to scatter crumbs over anyone sitting nearby. But the criticism seems nitpicking to me.

These are the principal crumble styles used by 96.7 percent (according to a recent poll) of all cracker users. The alternative cracker-breakers include those who break up the crackers inside those little sealed plastic restaurant servings before opening the package. Effective but boring. A few avant-garde crumblers have adopted what they consider esoteric means of breaking crackers; those mostly are considered smart alecks only interested only in fadism. One attempts to quarter crackers with a pair of tiny, silver scissors. Another uses the blunt end of a hunting knife, pounding the cracker on the table.

Most people nowadays are aware that cracker crumbling is a practice fully recommended by doctors and endorsed by the AMA. The reason, I believe, is obvious. Unsoftened cracker slivers are sharp and may cause internal damage. Most any doctor or nutritional scientist will tell you a sharp-edged cracker shard can harm the innards in a painful and ultimately expensive way. Many HMOs are considering saltines off-limits to curb soaring medical costs. So, medically speaking, crumbled crackers soften in the soup or chili and are a healthful benefit. Remind everyone to crumble when they need to, just to blunt this trend against it, if indeed what I saw was the beginning of a drift toward a no-crumble society.

The woman I watched didn't seem to know any better, more's the pity. It's possible she douses her hamburger in ketchup and eats fried chicken with a knife and fork, not her fingers, as is the practice. She was dining alone. I suspect she will experience many lonely dinners until she crumbles. We can only hope she comes to her senses in time.

%&@!# and Stones

May %&@!#

My Bones

Warning: cuss words ahead. That cautionary note is necessary for the few readers who continue, against all current practice, to complain that formerly dirty words are now commonly seen and heard everywhere.

That cussing has gone public here near the end of the twentieth century simply is the natural evolution from a hundred years of societal oppression and censorship that began in the blue-nosed Victorian period. It was the openness of the 1960s, of course, that broke barriers guarding dirty words in our language and spawned flower children, now Baby Boomers who have taken their unaffected speech into middle-American culture. They were the dirty-word groundbreakers who gave us, among other matters of etymological progress, T-shirts emblazoned with no-holds-barred messages. Thank you, one and all.

Back then, I noted the trend of more public cussing, commented on it, and praised the new Age of Aquarius conversational liberties. Today, all language obstructions are gone, and I believe it is a positive step forward. We were hypocritical, let's admit that. Now we know that once a dirty word is openly used repeatedly, it ceases being a dirty word. It merely is a word.

With our new freedom, it's not unusual to hear _____ and _____ spoken by the most discerning of persons. Those once forbidden words (and their rejoinder, _____) now are freely used in open society without a whit of embarrassment.

Accepting dirty words removes their shock value. If _____, _____, _____, or even _____ are public property, then no one feels offended by their use. Those 1960s pre-Boomers saw through the incongruity and paradox of _____ and _____ being hidden behind polite conversation and brought them into the sunshine. Naturally, in the beginning, adults were astonished to hear _____ but once said, the word's crudeness was ended.

The use of once-naughty terms and phrases, as _____ _____ and _____ _____, not to mention _____ _____, now is widespread and everyone says them regularly. I've heard a minister say _____ and a teenage girl reply _____ to a question. Women, old and young, utter _____ or _____ in mixed company. It's not unusual at all to hear elected officials say _____in their speeches.

When word censorship ended, newspapers, books, TV, and movies became much freer in their language. I remember when newspaper editors would remove _____ from a reporter's story, reasoning that even that relatively mild expletive would offend some readers. Probably you won't believe this, but one reporter recalls a particularly prudish editor who actually took out _____from a feature story. The reporter quit in protest, and I cannot blame him.

Language reticence is one thing, but not at the expense of our freedom of expression. Nowadays an author may say _____ when he means _____ and not have to substitute a euphemism or gentle word without the impact and descriptive value of _____.

The final dirty word to gain admission to society was, as you know, _____, though still there are people who are against its use. It's become a common, even clichéd term, in movies. Not long ago we published a well-researched and scholarly treatise on _____ and received several critical letters from readers. That's the price we pay for being on the cutting edge of language evolution, and we won't draw back from that responsibility. If you analyze _____ carefully, it is no more vulgar than _____ or _____, or _____. Nevertheless, it still has its detractors. I think I first heard it spoken aloud at a party, by a soft-voiced young woman. It brought gasps from listeners, then an embarrassed silence, and, finally, laughter when everyone realized that _____ was just another word. That rampart had been breached.

This public use of formerly dirty words has given us a new maturity and a fuller language with which to communicate with one another. Some of you may yet disagree. If so, then all I can say to you is _____.

A Dance
Of Myth
and Mane

This act of cutting—watched from a distance—seems an artless thing, unremarkable, even timeworn, a function of measured detachment, neither defining nor purposeful. It seems . . . ordinary.

There is no real beginning as in, say, rodeo, whatever the event, with horse and rider bursting, erupting, into an arena. For cutting, there is only the step-out, the first forward, often awkward and ungainly, stride of the horse, taken unceremoniously as a march of departure, not one of action. Reins are pleated through the rider's fingers and held with a facile indifference, upper body settled into a cutter's slump, and the sounds are like no others: the timorous pealing of bit and bridle, the scrunching of saddle leather, the restrained cadence of hooves. They only walk, man and animal, and about now, within the fixed rite of modern cutting, is a moment of premonition, of tension which comes sometimes with anticipatory silence. Sometimes it comes with what seems a collective intake of breath held until the horse crosses the time line, advancing on the massed and unmoving cattle.

So the drama begins. . . . And it is a *drama*, a staged performance played out in several brief, now and then fitful, acts, but there is little grand art in it for cutting is a craft of doing a learned and repetitive thing in a theatrical way.

Cutting actually is a worn shard of history; what we witness in a modern cutting arena is the ephemeral re-creation of a freedom; what we feel is the myth of time and ancientness and vanished absolution. Cutting comes from a long-ago age in which there were few metaphysical, and no literal, fences to living, a place of unclaimed pastures and unlimited horizons and men and horses who were as aboriginal as the plains they roamed.

The horses arrived with the Spaniards, though there are earlier equine roots than Andalusia—every cutting horse of the 1990s has stallion ancestors staked beside black tents in the deserts of Arabia. The conquistadors explored what now is West Texas and thought it "a wandering land," and *"La cola del mundo"*—the tail end of the world. A few Spanish horses escaped and grew into wild herds; "mustangs," those feral, shaggy-maned beasts were called. And there were Iberian cattle ranging free. The next men who came—and in the beginning there were almost no women—captured the mustangs, took skills and garb from the Mexican vaquero, and herded the cattle, becoming cowboys. It is this cult of the cowboy, of man on horseback (*"a' caballo,"* say the Spanish) that cutting celebrates, and it is such a simple thing: man and horse separate—"cut"—a cow from its herd, perhaps the most elemental, and necessary, of prairie skills. The psychology of this ingenuous act, though, is much more complicated, involving as it does the primitive relationship between man and horse. Together, they proclaim a remarkable symbiosis—"Pard-like" was J. Frank Dobie's phrase.

Cutting seems a most democratic and classless pastime. Riders can be, and are, of any gender and age, hewn from every socioeconomic peg on the scale. Horses, whether thoroughbred or mongrel, must have instinctive cow sense and some adequacy of quickness. That is all—that and practice, some luck, an agreeable cowherd. Together, they can do what neither is capable of alone; science calls that *synergy*, a rare catalytic force of nature. This remarkable symbiosis—the studied covenant—is essential to cutting, the rider urgent and aggressive without directing, the horse anticipating, intellectually and physically controlling the cow by knowing instinctively its next gambit.

The drama begins with the first separation, and then, quite often, comes the eyeblink-quick back and forth dance—a kind of prairiescape *pas d'cowpen*—between horse and cow. The rider has surrendered the reins, clutches, and pushes against the saddle horn, giving over command to the horse. In the best of these, the horse's *runic danse* is emphatic and turbulent—head down, ears flattened, legs splayed, body leaned at impossible angles ("rolling over the hocks," as cutters say), committing that prancing, muscular, dusty ballet, until the cow surrenders its will to man and horse.

And that is all cutting is, but within the context of that sudden explosive dance, what appears to be ordinary, is, in the doing, harmoniously *extraordinary*. In a world increasingly complex and hostile, cutting seems a kind of transient reiteration and observance of what was. It is, briefly, the recapturing of a lost freedom. So, there is no art in cutting, not in the *doing* of it. The art is in the memory and mythology, in the momentary re-creation of a long-ago time.

More
Do-Si-Do Than
Pas de Deux

I haven't understood a top ten song lyric since 1965. I'm certain the singers are saying something because their lips move, but only now and then do words come through, and never intelligibly—they always sound like "Hokapeigtwubabysvcipkgosuprak."

Mostly the lyrics are smothered by booming drums and jet-motor guitar screeches flowing from amplifiers the size of refrigerator crates. When I've complained about this, the raucous music overpowering lyrics, I've been told words are unessential to modern music. What matters is the beat, and can you fling your singular self around a dance floor to it? Dancing partners are optional. The idea is to express yourself in a way that anthropologists would consider primitive and tribal.

Now and then, the music decelerates and dancers engage in what they call "slow dancing," as though it is a physical therapy for retards. They are not very good at slow dancing, and movements are awkward, jerky. Young dancers today have no grace or elegance in gliding across the floor because, I think, girls have little practice at dancing backwards, and they are particularly resistant to anything in which boys lead. A waltz is beyond their comprehension.

Fortunately, understandable lyrics and partner dancing continue in the musical subculture we call country-western. The dance is a sort of prairie *pas de deux* called the two-step, so ubiquitous to our heritage that it's mostly known as the Texas Two-Step. Its origins come from frontier days when ranch dances were the only entertainment available for families.

"The Texans," observed visiting English woman Mary Jaques in 1893, "cannot be described as graceful dancers although they have some power of expressing the poetry of motion; their figures are supple, and they swing and sway a great deal. . . ."

Miss Jaques attended a ranch dance in central Texas and was properly courted and two-stepped by the cowboys. That was the two-step venue, ranch and farm houses, and cowboys would come from everywhere just to dance. ("Rode 20 miles, danced all night, rode 20 miles back," reads an 1881 diary entry of a cowboy who met his future wife at a ranch dance.)

Dances moved from house to house, perhaps by agreement, and rotated about every three months. Families came in wagons and buggies, men by horseback. Babies slept clustered in one big bed, young children played on the front porch, fiddles and guitars tuned up, dancing—or "daincing," as it was pronounced in Texanese dialect—commenced, usually not ending until dawn.

Two evolutionary results of ranch dances were (1) the economy of movement (there simply was no space in the small rooms for long-distance dancing), and (2) hatless two-stepping cowboys (it was poor manners to wear your hat in somebody's house).

Bob Wills, an inventor of western swing, remembered playing fiddle at age ten to his father's guitar in a home hallway while dancers two-stepped in every surrounding room. Wills boasted, proudly, that he never played or recorded a song that could not be two-stepped or waltzed to. He knew his roots.

Ranch dances ended as towns grew and public drinking was allowed in Texas. Beer joints were places young men and women could go weekly to meet one another.

Into this century, two-step dancing found sanctuary and salvation in the honky-tonks of mostly dry West Texas. Many a boy first danced in public at a beer joint, and early on whole families came, a holdover custom from the ranch dance days. And still men danced without their hats.

Looking back, it seems eighteen in Texas was the proper age to dance in public, meaning at a beer joint. I was eighteen, finally, and the beer joint was full and boisterous. It was Saturday night and she was much older, womanly, perhaps twenty-five, someone's sweetheart or wife or daughter who agreed to dance with me while he—a largish dour man leaning against the bar—watched. The music, I remember, came from two unamplified guitars, a fiddle, and a scarred upright bass. We two-stepped.

A rigid etiquette governed this coming-of-age ceremony, while dancing in public with someone else's woman, and I certainly observed it—my left hand cupped as a rest, not a grip, for her right hand, my free right arm around her but the hand held well above any notion of impropriety, our bodies almost but not quite touching. We spoke little because he was watching and familiarity bred fistfights. We danced once and I returned her to him and found other women, all with hims, either blood or choice, and when it was all over that night, I felt, well, manly.

I can't remember not knowing how to two-step. Born Texans seem still to know innately how to two-step. The man leads, the woman follows, and the movements are step left, step right, step left, hold briefly, step right, hold briefly, repeat. Traditional two-step developed, my theory goes, because it is suited to fiddle and guitar music played two-four time with a firm beat. *One-two, one-two, slide-shuffle.* And it is a dance that requires little space, though there can be considerable roundabout motion and stationary turning. The foxtrot, a four-four-beat ballroom dance, grew in the 1920s from the frontier two-step.

Today, an industry has sprung up to teach those without the dance in their DNA makeup. Lessons seem inordinately complicated for what is a simple dance, because many classes teach two-step as a kind of choreographed ballroom aerobics with elaborate movements called "patterns."

A sample "pattern" from a class sheet I saw read: "CLSD+(RDAbout Turn)+Step in front, RLOD)+(Step Back, Lead lady Pass By+(1 1//2 LOT+ SWHRT." My lord, it's only a little-bitty two-step dance, not "Swan Lake."

Real beer joints are about gone, replaced by less convivial bars with dance floors. The music remains C/W and, however loudly electrified, dancible. Lyrics can be understood. Young men, no longer in someone's home, dance with their hats on, and probably feel no need at eighteen for a formal passage into manhood. The two-step is still done, but loosened from the claustrophobic limits of ranch rooms and beer joints, it can cover a full dance floor. However grotesquely transformed here in the 1990s, the Texas Two-Step mostly is the dance of choice wherever fiddle music dominates and lyrics can be understood. And I've noticed one more thing: couples hold each other closer because there is no he watching by the bar. I was always in favor of closer dancing.

I recall a poetry snippet (perhaps it was a country song verse) that serves almost as an epitaph for the old Texas Two-Step dancing days:

> *Do I believe in dancing!*
> *Well, I should say I do;*
> *I'd ride the Devil's Highway*
> *To knock a step or two . . .*

The devil, in my memory, was an agreeable and lively dancing partner, but he always wanted to lead.

Death

And Extra

Innings

Much of my friend's story is a familiar one. First was a mild stroke which left him shaken but mostly intact, then a moderate heart attack, and another, followed the Big One, post-midnight emergency surgery, and her before-dawn telephoned voice, tearful but relieved, "He's OK. . . ." Prognosis, she was told, is better than just good. Perhaps his survival and prospects are, beyond the surgeons' skills, even providential. "He . . . died," she said, "but they brought him back." *A miracle.*

It was days before I could speak with him, and his voice was stronger than I expected, almost buoyant, "I'm up walking, sore but I can still walk. Should get out of here tomorrow, or next day." We talked awhile, then there was a long silence and he said, "I died, actually died on the table." *I heard.*

"You don't understand. I *remember* dying. . . . I saw myself die."

A near-death experience, this one with an out-of-body

event, both reported so frequently since the New Age came upon us that true believers have reduced such episodes to coded initials: NDE and OBE. They are the stuff of those odious tabloid TV shows, fodder for the *National Enquirer.* Writers have made millions relating these adventures beyond the pale, but none offers unimpeachable evidence that they actually happened.

Skeptical by nature and certainly by training, I am suspicious of what cannot be proven (and so was my friend, until now). To me, a near-death experience rates beside such cultural mythologies as kidnappings by extraterrestrials and Congress balancing the budget. Real science doesn't think much of NDE or OBE either. Both are subjective experiences defying scientific examination. Just once I wish some NDE subject would bring back soil samples or Polaroids.

The stories have an ubiquitous sameness: "floating above," an all-encompassing whiteness, the "tunnel," a single glaring source of light, ethereal music, a blue lake. Sometime faceless people are seen or persons identifiable but long dead. Many offer their NDE as proof of heaven; others think it certifies the realness of the human soul. Science guesses an NDE is an ambiguous deception of the brain, a false dream conjured up in times of stress, an escape strategy against high anxiety.

"Suddenly," my friend began, "I was floating, looking down at my body. I could see the surgeons and the machines, even dust on the light fixtures, and me . . . dead. I knew I was dead, and I knew I shouldn't be, that I wouldn't really die." Then slowly he was surrounded by whiteness, "the whitest white I have ever seen, and far away, a huge bright light, like a sun. I heard music. It was tuneless but pleasant to hear. I felt contentment for the first time in years.

"I began moving. I wasn't walking or running. It didn't

even feel like I was floating. I was just moving. I wanted to go to that sun. The whiteness had no dimensions, everything was white everywhere, but I felt like I was in a chute, a tunnel aimed at the light. I couldn't see a tunnel but there was one and I moved through it, listening to the music, staring at the light, not afraid at all.

"I heard voices ahead, getting louder. Then I was on the edge of a large lake, the water was perfectly flat and calm and a deep, deep blue. Across the water I could see people but their faces were shadowed by the sun behind them.

"Then I was in the water moving, not swimming, but just moving toward the other shore and the people. The water felt warm and comforting. I was near shore when I realized they were all men.

"One by one, their faces came into focus and I realized I knew them, knew all of them and knew, was absolutely sure, they were dead. They looked dead, acted dead. I had no uncertainty at all. They were dead."

He paused for the longest moment, then added: "It was the Texas Rangers."

There you have it. Finally, scientific proof of an NDE. *The Rangers are most decidedly dead, on earth as in heaven.* But then, so are the Dallas Mavericks, and their season hasn't even started yet.

East
Texas
Brigadoon

Somewhere in East Texas is my Brigadoon, a forested version of that magical Scottish town that appears just once each 100 years. Every year when fall arrives I think about it, where it is, and why I have never been able to find it again. I remember it and the day I spent there decades ago, as one of the most pleasant places and times of my life. Why can't I find it again?

That autumn I was driving through southern East Texas on a crisp morning when leaves were copper and orange, and I arrived in the small town. There was, in the approach, a morning hangover of ground fog swirling from a forest creek, and I came through the mist onto the town's symmetrical square. The courthouse was a Gothic creation, enormous and roughened by a hundred years of exposure to the weather. Around the courthouse was a square faced with old wooden storefronts. Huge oaks shaded the courthouse lawn, and there were benches for sitting.

Later in the day the lawn was filled with old men. They pitched horseshoes, played dominoes, or sat quietly on the worn benches, talking, warming in the soft lemon-colored sunlight. It was a scene of such pastoral simplicity that it could have been a painting. Throughout the day, people came and left the square, moving in a slow-motion pace, calling to one another, standing in clusters, talking. Late in the afternoon, after school, children arrived. There were boys with dogs, and girls in starched dresses, and they played on the courthouse lawn among the old men with their horseshoes and small talk.

I remember a grocery store, dimly lighted, and smelling of potatoes and onions, and the man behind the single counter passing bits of hard candy to the children. And there was a dry goods store, with shelves of work clothes, and tables of cloth wrapped in bolts, and the shop's owner who left for while at mid-morning, calling to his only customer, "If you find something, leave the money on the cash register. I'm going for a cup of coffee."

I ate lunch at the cafe. It had wooden tables with checkered cloths over them, rickety chairs, and a menu scribbled on a blackboard. Later I took dessert—a dish of ice cream served in one of those metal saucers—at the square's drugstore. The drugstore had a marble counter and stools that swiveled, and its wooden walls were plastered with cigarette posters and cosmetic circulars and there were patent medicines on shelves.

I left at near sunset, after the old men and children had deserted the courthouse lawn and never returned.

To this day, I cannot remember the town's name, though I can recall everything about it. I have driven many miles in East Texas searching for it, have found other towns with other courthouses and other old men but never my town, my Brigadoon. And each fall when leaves begin to color, I think of it, recall its placid, ancient square. I would like to see it again, just once.

Welcome to
Culture Gulch

We came in once a year like others living out there in the west, perennials in old cars with fresh cow or crop or egg money in our pockets. "Going to Cowtown," everyone said, explaining that annual journey down U.S. 80, the Mother Road from West Texas into Fort Worth.

Not so long ago, it was much like a seasonal migration: off the dry, high plains West Texans came, through the timbered Brazos bottomlands, over the western hills, then onto the bricked roadway of a magisterial double-wide boulevard called Camp Bowie with its antique lights and sentinel trees, across the Trinity and, finally, in among the tallest buildings between Dallas and the far left-hand margin of America.

Then "Going to Cowtown" was a habit because supplies were needed, or livestock had to be sold, or simply as relief from the lonesomeness of West Texas, and because Fort Worth was the nearest city with brighter lights, still raw and unfinished well into this century, both a cow town and a cowboy town by historic custom and inclination, comfortably western and unprepossessing. It was like home, only bigger, blessed with a comfortably plain-folks society always, as someone once wrote, "just one generation removed from flour-sack underwear."

Now they come from all directions because Fort Worth is keeper of the myths, and if one is to find any testimony to a surviving cowboy laity in Texas, Fort Worth is the place to look—though the search will turn up a severe dichotomy of purpose, and a mixed-breed culture, both high and low, like knowing which French wine to serve with chicken-fried steak. (The answer, of course, is a Bordeaux "rouge," preferably the '69.)

The one absolute fact of Fort Worth is that it "feels" like Texas should, or as outsiders want Texas to feel, which is the same thing. And if the cowboy myth often becomes entangled with the modern reality, so be it.

It is this almost playful lumping together of what is and what was—classical pianist icon Van Cliburn and seminal jazz saxophonist Ornette Coleman are as much cherished as Bob Wills, whose swing beat invented a whole new genre of country/western music—which sets Fort Worth apart: grand opera and horse operas riding the same trail; Bach and brahmas; a nice "Boeuf a la mode" and a mess of calf fries.

We may as well begin on a sunny afternoon from the plaza of the Amon Carter Museum, and the Japanese family outfitted in cheap felt western hats and necklaces of Nikons. They are photographing each other before the surrealistic Thomas Moore statuary, behind them the half-barrelled roof profile of the Kimbell Museum, city skyline in the distance, Camp Bowie Boulevard—still bricked—on the left, Will Rogers auditorium/coliseum/stock barns complex to the right.

No other spot so defines the seemingly off-hand coupling of traditional and modern Fort Worth. The sleek Moore statues are counterbalanced by the equestrian figure of Will Rogers, the cowboy humorist, resting on the lawn across the street. The Amon Carter Museum houses one of the world's finest collections of western art by Remington and Russell. The Kimbell simply is an American treasure, its Louis Kahn-designed building as much an art piece as the Picassos, El Grecos, Monets, and other grand paintings inside.

Near the Carter is the Modern Art Museum, which specializes in contemporary works from artists like Warhol and Pollock, and next door, the Museum of Science and History is a hands-on place with a planetarium and Omni theater. Both are in sight of the barns where cows and sheep and goats are housed for the annual stock show and rodeo, and the new equestrian center built for fine-breed exhibits and cutting horse competitions—all of this near Casa Manana, the musical theater in the round.

The equestrian center is pertinent to the history of this mild hill, which, in the 1890s, was a horse ranch, and that is the incongruous makeup of Fort Worth—you can't quietly sop up the city's "haute couture" without tripping over its cowboy roots.

Go wander through the Kimbell's current collections, but know that, outside, Butterfield stagecoaches once passed on their way to California long before impressionism was an artistic movement. Inspect the museum's incomparable works, but look west, too, to the hill's crown and understand that here was the Chisholm Trail, up which several million Longhorns were herded to Kansas railheads.

Beside this cultural district, cavalry soldiers went west to battle Indians, and buffalo hunters lumbered by in their heavy wagons, and settlers went out to homestead land given them by Texas—a couple of generations later, their descendants, now Joads of the Prairie, began coming back in their once-a-year Diaspora, "Going to Cowtown," seeking diversion and culture, and maybe a hundred-pound sack of flour and new school clothes, a house dress for mama, a cool straw western hat for daddy.

Cowboys herding their cattle through Fort Worth always passed a few recreational nights in Hell's Half Acre, a downtown district of saloons and gambling joints and rentable women. The Acre was near today's brick-streeted Sundance Square, where nights still are recreational, but far more sedate—the attraction now is cafes and bars, theaters (both stage and cinematic), another cache of Remington and Russell paintings in the Sid Richardson Collection of Western Art, the inscrutable Caravan of Dreams, which presents—no question about this—the best jazz music in America.

A new performing arts center is downtown, not far from where once was a saloon in which cowboys were allowed to ride their horses up to the bar, and where regional bad guy Sam Bass bought all his bank robbing supplies, and where Sam Houston's youngest son, Temple, a lawyer and fast gun, often played poker, sometime, legend insists, wearing a dead rattlesnake for a hatband. Another legend says Bonnie and Clyde, who also robbed banks, drove their Model A Ford sedan down Main Street, circled the courthouse, and went north over the Trinity, where they spent the night in the Stockyards Hotel.

Perhaps not. The good thing about legends is they don't have to be true, only believable. What is true is that the Stockyards is the core of Fort Worth's western persona.

What a few years ago was not worth tearing down now is

a National Historic District and the first destination of all those outsiders "Going to Cowtown" in search of cowboy-ism at its most intense.

Long before tourists arrived, many of the stores along Exchange Avenue were peddling western wear and ranch supplies, its restaurants were dishing up calf fries and well-done T-bone steaks, its musicians were fiddling, because the customers were West Texans and the Stockyards was a way of life, not a marketing campaign.

The Stockyards are authentic, down to the remaining cattle pens and Livestock Exchange, the old barns, the Swift and Armour plants, the ancient coliseum in which the world's first indoor rodeo was performed.

Rodeos, and other cowboy riding events, still are staged in the coliseum, cattle auctions still go on in the Exchange building—though now they're likely to be televised and featuring exotic livestock such as emus, not Longhorns. The Stockyards trade now depends on outsiders, who come for the western essence—and they find it in Billy Bob's Texas, in which the biggest stars of country music perform, in the sight and sound of the ancient Tarantula steam train, in the $500 custom-made boots and $95 plastic steer horns suitable for mounting and the $6 plates of barbecue. None of this especially is high-brow and elitist, and in the Stockyards, it's difficult to find the contrast of cultures that modern Fort Worth endures, though there is a precedence there for it.

In the coliseum, in 1920, Caruso performed before 7,000 people for the largest single concert fee he ever received, a reported $10,000. That he was singing in a rodeo arena was contradictory enough, but the *Fort Worth Star-Telegram* reported that he entered the coliseum through a rear door and up a cattle ramp. This greatest of operatic tenors eyed the ramp, bowed his shoulders, bellowed like a Longhorn, and charged into the building—then stopped and grinned for reporters, acknowledging his little western joke. At the conclusion of Caruso's concert, finishing his encore aria, *"Noche Feliz,"* the tuxedoed and ball-gowned audience stood and cheered, almost afrenzy with the fustian ecstasy of it all when—wrote the *New York Times* critic—a cowboy seated high in the stands yippeed, threw his hat in the air, and fired off his six-guns.

That certainly was an intrinsic, defining Fort Worth moment in history—six-guns and sonatas—and the essential experience outsiders look for. Come any summer day to the Stockyards and there they are, visitors from everywhere including places where other languages are spoken. They wander the brick streets, petting the horses ridden by policemen, being photographed in the saddle strapped on the back of a thoroughly bored Longhorn steer, absorbing the westernality by osmosis and message T-shirts. They buy the cheap hats and jeans and boots, and the legends. For a little while, they are cowboys.

Certainly that Japanese family in the cultural district believed themselves to be cowboys. From the Amon Carter Museum, they crossed the street and posed one another against Will Rogers' statue. One child hung onto the neck of Will's horse—its name, for the record, is Soapsuds—and slung off his new cowboy hat, yelling "Yip-pee," which amazingly sounds the same in Japanese as in Texan.

And that may be Fort Worth's most gratifying contribution to this whole western thing. We allow people, for a little while, to play cowboy. Doesn't matter who you are, an Italian tenor or a '90s band of samurais, come to Fort Worth and you get to play cowboy. It's an old tradition.

Before "Dominoes"
Meant Pizza

My dominoes are inherited, a family heirloom in an oblong, aged red-and-white box emblazoned with a stalwart American eagle—wings spread, beak raised nobly, talons clutched onto a double-six, the emperor gladiator of the domino world. Magna Dominoes are a product, the box says, of the Milton Bradley Company, Springfield, Mass. This, the box proclaims rather grandly on two sides in bold script, is, "A Double Six Set with Rules," though printed game instructions that came with the box were lost long ago.

Whatever games were explained, I know 42 was not among them because (1) it essentially is a regional pastime and (2) the recently published *Winning 42: Strategy and Lore of the National Game of Texas,* by Dennis Roberson (Lubbock: Texas Tech University Press), is the first book of official playing instructions and strategies in its long century-old history. That's an amazing thing that says more about the rural Texas culture in which it was invented than 42 itself. Its rules and skills were passed through oral tradition, like family history, and 42's lineage is so pure that the way the game was played originally in 1887 is about the way it's played today. There are variations, especially beyond Texas (Cajun Hokey Pokey comes to mind), a few bidding adjustments (like Nel-o and Plunge, which purists sneer at), even a kind of black sheep relative called Moon (players often gamble at this, which clearly was not what 42's Baptist inventors intended—42 came into being because card-playing was considered sinful; dominoes weren't).

But mostly 42 as it is today is what it always was—less a game than a rural social pastime, as necessary and productive as community quiltings or the shelling of black-eyed peas on the front porch by neighborhood women passing hot late-summer afternoons. It was a homemade socialization tool in a time when people had to entertain themselves.

Thursday was 42 night at my house. Whole families came. The women brought covered dishes, the children their energy and noise. We ate. Women cleaned away the plates and bowls. Men set up the tables, arranged chairs, and shooed the kids into back rooms, or if it was warm, outside. The game began. Sometime it was one table, sometimes as many as four; always it was part gossip, part banter, part clicking and slapping of dominoes and genial arguing over tricks and marks— "Cecil pencil-whipped us when we wasn't lookin'," I remember a player alibing, meaning that the scorer purposely miscalculated. The fun would go on until all hours, often as late as 9:30 P.M.

Mine was an ordinary 42 experience in any small Texas town. Home 42 parties were endemic in those days, but there were other, almost always male-only, places to play. I remember a regular game at the feed store behind the cheese factory. For awhile there even were domino tables set up in the pool hall, but that arrangement came to a tragic end.

Forty-two was played, but so was Moon, a three-player version of the game. Moon causes gambling in rascals and weaker men. One day in a two-bits-a-hickey Moon session, three old men argued, then fist-fought, and the town was only too happy to rush in and padlock the place; truthfully, the target actually was the pool games. Pool was believed to induce loafing in young men, who then fell to smoking ready-rolls, which, without question, led directly and inevitably to—and the Baptists had anecdotal evidence validating this—dancing. Sin was much more obvious and linear back then.

At one time almost every small town in Texas featured a domino parlor, which served as a male social center. Boys could come in, but females were discouraged because their presence severely impaired a player's obligation to cuss his luck or a partner's play. Besides, women could play at the home 42 parties and that was enough. Public 42 was man's work.

The irony of 42's invention as a permissible substitute for wicked card playing—it most resembles bridge or the English card game of whist (and variants like pitch or euchre)—was that it could be played on rural front porches after church services, after Sunday dinner, with neither shame nor sin. It showed up at the social proceedings after river baptisms and was a staple pastime for community cemetery workings, for which people gathered yearly to clear family burial plots of weeds, followed by dinner on the ground and games.

Over in the secular world, 42 was played wherever men gathered, in the sodality of ranch bunkhouses, hunting and fishing trips (on river banks, 42 was illuminated by coal-oil lantern light and interrupted while somebody went off periodically to run a trot line), and at oil well sites. Most general stores had a domino table set up back by the wood stove. After the game went urban, workers in heavy industry warehouses ate their lunchbox sandwiches during noontime 42 games. At Fort Worth's big airplane factory, dozens of 42 tables were played before and after shift changes, a few with dominoes made from scrap aluminum used to build B-29 bombers. Oil-field roughnecks often had to live at the well sites in remotest West Texas, and their off-hours recreation was 42. "Regular dominoes was a kind of sissy game," recalled a retired pumper, meaning his bunch considered 42, which requires sly strategy and aggressiveness, a manly activity.

I remember a highway hamlet—just a grocery store, a one-chair barbershop, and filling station—with its ongoing Saturday afternoon game. The loafers played under the shady filling station canopy, their table an old metal Quaker Oil sign laid over a barrel. There was a Coke box cooled by block ice and a rack holding nickel-a-package Tom's Salted Peanuts. On a graveled strip beside the station, other loafers waiting their turn at the 42 table pitched washers to pass the time. To this day, I can hear the rhythmic shurring of dominoes being shuffled on that steel oil sign and the loud clank of a high trump domino being slammed down in celebration. "Gimme that five-four," somebody would shout, slamming ("Clang!") the double-five and cackling in his triumph. Sometimes the game would become so involved and raucous people had to pump their own gas.

Not long ago I got lost in East Texas, down by Votaw. It was my own fault. The azaleas were blooming and the magnolias, and on a late spring morning I turned onto a dirt road through the pines, and another, and another until I had no sense of where I was, not that it mattered much. Finally, I found a hot-top road and took it for a mile or two until I crossed over a hill and down into a town. The square was busy. It was Saturday and folks were in for their shopping, their pickups and old cars nosed into the spaces around the turreted red-stone Romanesque courthouse. Kids were playing on the courthouse lawn, and over under the trees were old men around domino tables, unmindful that their 42 game and the courthouse were relics of the nineteenth century, that this pastoral scene a hundred years later had hardly changed over the years.

What was, is, and 42 is still around, still played by tens of thousands of people. There are 42 parties, though not as many or as often, and it is less a social pastime now than a casual recreation. Texas still has domino parlors here and there. There are tournaments, even state champions, not a few of whom have been female; the domino hall walls have been breached.

Forty-two lives on, and here, finally, is an official book of rules and strategies, its history and folklore and tales from the tables by those who have kept the game going.

Any pastime invented to avoid sinning is still worth doing. Go ye and do likewise.

Shades

Of

Yesteryear

Now and then around the Texas countryside, old gray, empty houses can be seen in fields, all the living gone from them. If of a certain pre-World War II age, though, these abandoned homes each have a common architectural characteristic. They have front porches. To explain front porches, their social value, to a modern generation accustomed to indoor living with air-conditioning and backyard concrete patios is not an easy matter. They don't understand. You had to be there, must have sat on one to appreciate it, and few do that any more.

Architecturally, a porch was practical in hot Texas, the South and Southwest, because it provided a shady barrier to help cool the house. Porches were covered areas attached to houses. Most were in front but some stretched around each side and a few homes—the large elegant ones, mostly—had porches completely surrounding them. Depending on the size, neighborhood, area of the country, and social position of its owner a porch was called a porch, a verandah, portico, colonnade, even a stoa if the occupant had some knowledge of Greek or Latin. To be honest, porches were to houses what tail fins were to those old Buicks or cuffs to trousers. They had little or no value, except as ostentation, and were superfluous to the basic structure of most houses.

But their worth was immeasurable to society. Porches were a rural staple and probably more than any other single ingredient typified that now almost-vanished piece of Americana called the small town. Porches, you see, were gathering grounds. Whole families would sit on them. Neighbors would amble over from one house to another, just to sit awhile on a front porch. They were cool on late summer afternoons and you could sit and catch whatever breezes happened by.

Porches were sat on at two principal times. Mostly they were used in evenings, at sunset and twilight, but Sundays after lunch—lunch was called "dinner" then—families would come and rest awhile. It was after church, after good clothes had been changed, after fried chicken had been done away with. The men came out first, while the women cleared the kitchen, and they would sit there and not say much of anything, except maybe "Oh lordy, I'm full." Then one by one they would rise from the rocking chairs and go inside for a nap.

People were more talkative in late afternoons, especially among neighbors who gathered on front porches. World problems were solved, gossip exchanged. Like the porches, though, conversation was itself useless and only important because it brought people together.

Porches had things on them. There were chairs, certainly a rocker or two, and a swing hung from two chains, coffee cans or Mason jars holding a favorite flower, and surely a thermometer given by the local funeral home was hanging near the front door. Across the ends of many front porches honeysuckle vines or climbing roses had been planted. In late spring honey bees and even butterflies found them, buzzing and fluttering in the twilight. These things made noises. Swings squeaked. Rocking chairs made mild thumps. Steps always groaned when you sat on them. The screen door—and houses had front screen doors in those pre-air-conditioned days—both squeaked and thumped. On especially hot evenings there was the rhythmic tattoo of a hand-turned ice cream freezer.

People sitting on porches looked out on things. They saw neighbors strolling by on sidewalks (sidewalks were strips of concrete running in front of houses, usually the length of entire blocks, and were perfect for skating or riding your bike on). Cars passed, and after dark came fireflies, like blips on a dark radar screen.

From the sidewalk you could pass in the night and hear a murmur of conversation from each porch. After radio became popular people propped their small sets in windows and sat on porches listening to their favorite programs. You could walk a block and never miss a word of *Amos 'n Andy* or *The Jack Benny Show*.

All of this is gone. Two declared world wars, especially the last one, killed the front porch, I think. In the mid-1940s there was a change in architectural styles. Pier-and-beam construction gave way to the more expedient concrete slab, this because quick boxy (and cheap) housing was needed to serve the thousands of people who moved to work in urban area war plants. Porches, not useful to the requirements of an eight-to-five shift at the bomber plant, were eliminated. After the war soldiers returned but not to the rural small towns they had left. They went to the big city and began making good money. More urban homes were needed and developers were quick to throw up cheap houses. Without porches, of course. Air-conditioning and television moved people inside and that was that. Front porches were gone forever.

Rear patios are a poor substitute for the old porches. They are concrete slabs hidden behind houses and fences, with little warmth and social comfort. You cannot see the world from rear patios and not often bees and butterflies, and out there a gallon of supermarket ice cream does not taste the same. There's no place to hang the mortician's thermometer, and rockers and swings have no sounds on concrete.

How Sweet
The
Sound

I heard it again last fall in the Ozarks late at night with the air crisp and smelling of hickory wood smoke from an open fire. The singing of it, the wondrous, evocative blending of words and melody, caused an immediate, commanding silence. It always does.

> *A-maz-ing grace,*
> *How sweet the sound*

The girl's voice was full and unaffected, and it came from beyond the bonfire's pocket of warmth and light. She sang with some inner long-remembered cadence, seamlessly crossing into the verse's final phrasing

> *But now I'm found*
> *Was blind, but now I see*

A fiddler picked up the melody line, and then came the rich tones of an old flat-head Martin guitar, and a thumping bass and two banjos, and someone else joined the singing, and others, until we were a choir and "Amazing Grace" grew verse after verse into a joyful crescendo.

It's just, of all things, an old church hymn, but I long ago decided it has a kind of canonical southernness that creates an unequivocal sense of place. In the South, where music is a geographical measure, "Amazing Grace" is a shared experience. I heard it this time in Mountain View, a snippet of an Arkansas town with a square of antique shops surrounding a bulky old courthouse. And before Mountain View, I had listened to "Amazing Grace" in eastern Tennessee, on a fresh spring morning that smelled of coffee and azaleas, frying ham and new grass, in a country church snuggled away at the end of a narrow valley. There was an aching beauty to the congregation's ingenuous singing of it, as there always is in rural churches.

My first memory of "Amazing Grace" was in a country church of North Texas. Shaded by cottonwood trees, it was small and white, this church, with long, hard benches made by the men and a simple oak lectern from which the preacher, who often took his pay in chickens and roasting ears, called for a finish to sin. "Amazing Grace" was performed often enough for me to remember all five verses, and it was best done on hot summer Sunday mornings when the church's windows were raised and voices spread out into the countryside.

"Amazing Grace" was the song my grandmother hummed as she quilted or shelled early spring peas on the front porch or cooked sugar pies on her wood stove. It was her busy-time song, learned in her rustic nineteenth-century chinked-log church, the one in which she and my grandfather were married. The presence of "Amazing Grace" made her feel good, secure, was comforting and comfortable, and that is perhaps the song's most enduring quality. It was to her, and continues to be, a reaffirmation of the southern past.

Though I suspect many southerners, perhaps most of us, found "Amazing Grace" in church, the song long ago leaped the religious fence and became, if not quite secular, at least free and worldly enough for any occasion. In a bar serving as a wedding hall somewhere out in the southern Louisiana swamps beyond Bayou Vista, the rhythms were pure Cajun, the singer a roughneck from an off-shore oil rig, his voice cracking and untutored but somehow correct. Once I heard a country/western guitar player hush a raucous, beery crowd in a Nashville nightclub with his solo rendition of it, the chording and fingering sounding almost like a Mozart benediction.

A decade ago I boarded the Delta Queen in Memphis, partially because the old passenger sternwheeler is a floating relic and I like the genteel senescence of her but mostly because Willie Humphreys was playing jazz all the way to New Orleans. Willie's raspy clarinet still is performing, but then he was seventy and his music, with a half-century of hard living in it, was at once joyful and earthy and melancholy, as good jazz should be. Late one afternoon near Friars Point, beyond OK Bend, we were gathered on the Texas deck to watch sunset over the Mississippi delta and began talking about the blues, which Willie held a Ph.D. in, and somebody said blues, if executed properly, could make people feel good, and Willie agreed, and somebody else said blues was constrained within a narrow musical genre, and Willie said no it isn't, that blues wasn't notes and words, it was an emotion.

He picked up his clarinet, began playing, and the music was hard-core blues with a hoarse saloon texture whose tempo was set by the turning paddlewheel. "Amazing

Grace." The other musicians let Willie go it alone for a verse or two, then the trombone came in from a bottom slide, the trumpet took the high notes, and a banjo laid down a chorded percussion base, and most of us sang quietly,

> *'Twas grace that taught my heart to fear*
> *And grace my fears relieved . . .*

Later Willie said the man that wrote "Amazing Grace" surely knew sadness. Probably. Most certainly John Newton knew remorse. He was English, born in 1725, an illiterate commoner. Sent off to sea as a boy, he rose to the rank of captain. His trade was slavery, and he landed at least one cargo of human freight on the docks of Charleston, South Carolina. Then Newton went home to England, studied for the ministry, and became in 1764 the Curate of the Church in Olney, where he wrote what musical history calls The Olney Hymns, among them, "Amazing Grace." Which explains why once in the Scottish Highlands, I heard a lone bagpiper play the song I associated only with a small white church in Texas.

Fifty years later when the American South was being settled by emigrants from England and Scotland and Ireland, "Amazing Grace" came along as baggage, a Elizabethan stowaway with what would become the basis for all southern folk music.

Folk music took me to Mountain View. I crossed the Arkansas at Little Rock, and immediately left the interstate because an Ozarks autumn, with its red and brown and gold forests, should be seen from country roads through towns like Rose Bud and Ida and Timbo. Outside Mountain View is the Ozark Folk Center, a remarkable repository of music and a kind of national treasure dedicated to the preservation of southern folk crafts, especially music. Nightly, the music is performed in the huge auditorium as it has been for generations, plainly, simply, without amplification, just instruments and voices.

And later, if you are lucky, somebody will say, "Come on over to Charley's for the pickin'." Which is more music, but at someone's home. People come and bring dishes of food and their instruments and they play tunes they learned from their parents, who learned it from their parents, who perhaps brought it from England or Scotland.

I stood near the fire that crisp evening, listening to the old songs, like the fiddle-fancy "Indian on a Stump" and "Arkansas Traveler" and the banjo-driven "Cripple Creek," the bouncy "Sally Goodin'," to which several couples danced on the concrete garage floor. Then, long after midnight came the girl's loud, clear voice.

A-ma-zing grace, how sweet the sound

Very sweet, as always.

A Cowboy's
Kingly
Crown

I haven't worn Old Man Crow's hat in thirty years, maybe longer, but there it sits on a high bookshelf, stained, sweat-streaked, the tall crown deeply indented, the brim curled at its edges and darkened by age. It was ancient when Old Man Crow gave it to me but not as ancient as he, though both were well worn and long-used, each irrelevant to a modern world. He was at least seventy, three decades ago, a cowboy with nowhere left to cowboy, and the hat was a relic of the past, a kind of apparel fossil from a time and a place now measured by myths and legends.

The cowboy hat comes to us from out of American history as only one of two pieces of clothing that instantly identifies the work and character of their wearer: a cowboy hat is worn by a cowboy, and he is booted. With a tall-crowned hat and high-heeled boots, the wearer can only be a cowboy. Never mind that today hats and boots are mostly symbolic, an affectation for even country/western singers and "Montgomery Ward Cowboys," the latter once a scornful term for wannabes who outfitted themselves by mail order from that company's catalog.

Our western experience—ranches and ranchers, cowboys and cows—began in West Texas, and its required clothing and gear came from that worn and used by the Mexican vaquero, who was the first cowboy. The hat, whose form has changed little in a century and a half, evolved from the round, full-brimmed sombrero. Unlike other western wear, the authentic cowboy hat is identified with one man—John B. Stetson, whose last name became generic to his product. "Gettin' me a pair of striped pants and a Saturday night Stetson," explained one long-ago cowboy planning how to spend his cattle drive wages.

In the late 1860s, Stetson made the first cowboy hat of heavy felt, gave it the high crown, slightly curved-brim profile and named the model "Boss of the Plains." Texas Rangers immediately adopted the hat, and its use spread across the West. What cowboys had, though, was not just a hat with a distinctive shape; it was another working tool. Its most immediate use was as a fortification against weather: its brim shaded cowboy eyes from the heavy Texas sun; it was waterproof and shed rain; it was warm in winter (a cowboy could fold the brim down over his ears and tie it there with his kerchief to keep out the cold); during hot spells, it served as a handy fan. Rolled or folded, the hat formed a serviceable pillow. Many a horse ate oats or corn from a cowboy hat and drank water from it, too. One story tells of a cowboy crossing a long dry stretch of prairie. His canteen sprung a leak. He saved the drinking water by carrying it in his Stetson.

A cowboy could fight grass fires with it, swat balky cows or stubborn horses, beat the dust off his jeans. Racing to stop a runaway herd, a cowboy flung his hat at the lead steer. It sailed like a Frisbee into the steer, which, startled, turned and ended the stampede but not before every animal had run over and stomped the hat into a gray mass. The cowboy thumped up the crown with his fist, creased it with a rough forefinger, hand-curled the brim—and rode on, wearing his almost indestructible hat.

That was his weekday, working hat. His more expensive

Saturday night hat was a social expression and may have cost a month's wages. He danced with his Saturday night hat on and wore it when drinking in a friendly way but removed it for fights and kept it free of ornamental trimmings. Fancy-colored bands and feathers were considered effete, pretentious, unworthy of a real cowboy who didn't need add-ons to prove himself. So, of course, most modern cowboy hats are duded up with bands of exotic skins, bright feathers, even enameled pins.

My Saturday night hat has a plain band but is festooned with jaunty feathers, a garnish that would have embarrassed Old Man Crow. It is the finest of cowboy hats, a 4XXXX silver-belly beaver Shady Oak model blocked and trimmed by Peter Bros. Hats, which has been selling western headwear for eighty-three years in downtown Fort Worth. It was presented with a silver dollar, an old tradition connected with the purchase of a really fine western hat. I keep my hat in a plastic sack inside its Stetson box and only wear it for rodeos and stock shows and other western events that we Montgomery Ward cowboys dress up for.

The Stetson name on the sweatband inside Old Man Crow's working cowboy hat has faded with age, but it remains readable, proof of the hat's enduring quality. I've come to agree with one cowboy who wrote, "A Stetson will take on weight, and it will get to the point where you can smell it across the room, but you can't wear it out."

Long ago, an unknown cowboy poet jotted down a few verses in appreciation of his hat, four telling lines of which are:

> *Mistreated, abused on a roundup spree,*
> *Walked on, tromped on, old J.B.*
> *You've been a good pal through all of that,*
> *You dirty, old—gray, old—Stetson hat.*

Giddy
Up—
Way Up

We went up the mountain at midmorning after the sun had burned away the haze on Pine Top. Here in the Guadalupe Mountains, the trail up the canyon is narrow, level, and flanked by agave and sotol, hardly a trail at all. Mexican laborers using hand tools and courage cut the tight path decades ago. The horses were "rock horses" because they were experienced on the trail, but still their hooves slipped on the loose gravel and skidded over the stones.

From the ranch house to the crest of Pine Top Mountain, the canyon trail rises in cutbacks almost 4,000 feet. A dozen times it crosses the dry stream bed of the gorge, snakes behind the immense boulders that have fallen from the mountain, and climbs over rock ledges for which you must dismount and lead your horse. To the left is Guadalupe Peak, a mountain of little physical beauty. That it is Texas' highest point is the mountain's only distinction from afar. Behind us rose the blunt rock face of El Capitan, its white cliffs seen from fifty miles into the flatlands below. By any definition the bulk of El Capitan is a glorious sight and one of America's most dramatic natural landmarks.

Above the canyon the path becomes loosely packed gravel and sharp turns. You ride 300 feet to rise vertically by fifty feet. The horses slip in the gravel, which slides down the sharp mountainside. One horse falls to its knees, its hind legs hanging over the point of the trail. The rider jumps off, but the horse rears and falls on him. His head strikes a rock, and he is cut on each forearm by the stones. But he is safe and only bruised and dazed. As the injured rider remounts, someone says the trail seems dangerous now and the guide agrees.

An hour later, the trail tops out and we ride into a bowl, a depression on which a conifer forest grows. It is what scientists call a first-born forest, one thousands of years old. The forest is thick in the basin. Fir, ponderosa pine, oak, the red-skinned Texas madrone, a beautiful tree, and scattered maple saplings cause slow riding.

We eat lunch in a pine draw, out of the wind, and later ride to the mountain's edge. U.S. 180 can be seen from the mountain. It is a thread across the flat desert, heading west through the salt marshes to El Paso. The horizon is pale and dusty and the West Texas grasses are a poorly defined green, like algae on a dirty pond. Wreckage of a light plane lies on the side of a mountain across from us, in full sight of the highway and civilization. Yet searchers could not find the plane for thirty-one days after it crashed.

Guadalupe is more distinct from Pine Top and assumes a stance of unlovely grandeur. Somewhere on Guadalupe is a monument, a triangular memorial placed there years ago by American Airlines. Workers carried it to the mountaintop in three pieces and erected it in memorial to all airline pilots who fly over the peak. The scene from Pine Top is a sobering one. The Guadalupes may or may not become a national park [Editor's Note: they did]. Should legislative machinery ever act toward that end Pine Top, Guadalupe Peak, and the pristine majesty of McKittrick Canyon would be saved. No one disagrees that it should be protected. Opponents differ on how. As a mountainous area Supreme Court Justice William Douglas called it one of America's most rugged sections.

But it is more than that. Geologically and biologically it is unique and beyond duplication. For thousands of years the mountains and the canyons protected themselves by their distance and forbidding presence. Later, fortunately, enlightened men became caretakers, and the area has passed today with little changed in those thousands of years.

There are elk here. We see their droppings on the mountain. Wild turkeys, mountain lions, and black bears live in remote canyons. Wild hogs, released in southern New Mexico, are beginning to appear in the mountains.

In McKittrick Canyon are Texas' only native trout. The canyon almost cannot be explained fully. It, too, is a relic, a living antiquity. The creek, spring-fed, holds small pools in which the trout live, and is lined with juniper, the madrone, gray oak, fir, and the maple. There is a catholic silence, except for the creek's wanderings, bordered by a thin, worn trail used earlier by Indians—Apaches, mostly—who dared come into the mountains. Few reach McKittrick Canyon today. There is a rough dirt road, eight miles in length (which takes more than an hour to travel) leading from U.S. 180. To see the canyon you need keys for three locked gates and permission to enter. Perhaps within a decade the area will be a national park and all can enter. Perhaps not.

Before we leave Pine Top for the two-hour ride down the sharp, twisting trail, we ride back through the forest. For an instant, four deer, a buck, and two does followed by a younger, smaller deer, stand in a clearing. We watch through the trees. Then a horse snorts and the deer raise their tails, search into the wind with their noses, and run away into deeper regions of the bowl. When the deer are gone we ride out of the forest and down the mountain in late afternoon sunlight.

Makin'

Bacon

Long before pigs were household pets and movie stars, before chemicals could make dry turkey meat taste like lean bacon except when you're actually eating it, the onset of cooler weather brought about a need to go out in the backyard and kill something, usually a fat hog. Now that Texas is mostly urban and a right-to-carry state, we limit our backyard slaughter to bugs and crabgrass, and cities restrict what we can kill on our patios.

In Nashville this year, two women were fined for killing sheep behind their house. Recent arrivals from Afghanistan, they sacrificed the sheep in some type of religious ceremony, which offended neighbors, many of whom were preparing to barbecue dead meat because the day just happened to be July 4, a time when we commemorate our freedoms. In the writing business, we call this an ironic circumstance. Multiculturalism is a hard horse to ride when religious liberties conflict with municipal ordinance, even when sheep are involved. Why can't those Afghans be Christian-like and, as the Bible relates, just serve up a fatted calf for sacrifice—what else is patio barbecue but burnt offerings? (The Old Testament took no position on coleslaw and pinto beans but was bullish on chicken-fried manna from heaven.)

I have, I notice, swerved over into preaching as I headed off to explain cold weather and hog killing. An unorganized mind is easily led into irrelevant but provocative side-alleys, though I never really cared for sheep, anyway.

Hog killing was an annual organized social ritual when self-sufficiency was necessary in the countryside. It was a noun, as in "We're havin' a hog killin' Saturday. Come on over." And neighbors arrived to help. Sometimes the hog killing was a multi-family affair and everyone gathered their hogs at a central site for butchering and preparation of the meat. Whatever the scope, a hog killin' required many hands and much muscle, an entire day, and cold weather to keep the meat from spoiling. Usually, it was a kind of community party with a noontime feast, and, occasionally, music and dancing at night.

The children were there to help, but mostly they played with the pig bladders, which were similar to large balloons and could be batted around like volleyballs. We used to take them down to the creek and float them in the current, throwing rocks until someone scored a hit—the bladders would burst and sink. I doubt that a sheep's bladder is large enough for any fun activities, though I've never seen a sheep butchered and have no firsthand knowledge. I don't know any Afghans to ask. No sense inquiring around here. Texas raises more sheep than almost any region but eats less lamb and mutton than even, say, Eskimos.

I see that I've steered off into another unrelated cul-de-sac, but I believe I can get back to the subject by acknowledging that certain Eskimo tribes do eat the viscera of animals such as seals and whales.

In hog killing circles, the viscera (frankly, this is intestines and other pig parts, the porcine equal of homeopathic natural junk food) was both utilitarian—sausage could be stuffed into large intestine links—and sort of eerie hors d'oeuvres cooked and fed to workers by the host housewife. Back then, people actually ate pig livers, hearts, brains, knuckles (the ankles), feet, and the maw (don't ask). Ears and snouts were considered delicacies. If not served up individually, these parts were prepared as souse, which appears today under the alias "headcheese"—a gelatinous mass laced with bits of pig scraps. I'm pleased to say I've never eaten headcheese on purpose.

First, the hogs were slaughtered. Usually, this was done by a carefully placed .22 rifle shot behind an ear. The throat was slit, and the hog hung upside down to drain all blood. That's the messy part. The hog carcasses were dipped into boiling water to loosen hair, which was scraped off. Then the cutting began—hams, chops, bacon, ribs, all the good stuff. Fat was rendered into lard, both for cooking and making lye soap. Some meat was run through a muscle-cranked grinder for sausage. The sausage was mixed by hand with spices such as sage and cayenne pepper in galvanized washtubs. Either intestines—thoroughly cleaned and inverted—were used for storing sausage or the casings were made from flour sacks. Afterwards, all the meat cuts were stored in a smokehouse and literally smoked for weeks. Families needed those meats to carry them through cold winters.

Two other dishes came from the hogs. One was cracklings, which were leftover from the lard rendering process and were tasty and crunchy, often mixed into cornbread batter for flavoring. Cracklin' bread, it was called. The second was chitlins—we're back to small intestines again. Chopped and soaked in salt water, the fried chitlins were considered good eating. Strange to say, cracklin's are a packaged snack food today. One brand explains them as "Fried out pork fat with attached skin, salt added" and notes that cracklin's are "Not a Significant Source of Dietary Fiber," as though it mattered. Fried pork skins also are packaged and an avowed favorite of our last Republican president, Mr. Bush. His Ivy League upbringing allowed no experience with hogs and hog killing so we are left to guess where he picked up the habit of eating fried pig rinds. Could be he was after the Eskimo and Afghan voting blocs. If so, someone should have told him there are no pigs above the Arctic Circle and Afghans do not eat pork in any form.

As long as we're off onto a side trail again, you should know I think the sheep got what they deserved, July 4 or not. Baa, baa, bah.

The Lowdown

On

Hunkering

It's never easy being a distinguished pundit in this age of gross sensitivities. I intended to discuss the fine lost art of hunkering (with a subtext on the principles of Essence Repatterning) but almost immediately was thwarted by our policy of not writing _____. Instead, I'm forced to use "haunches," a crude though politically correct term, and necessarily gender neutral because the subject is unladylike in its practice and a custom considered ill-suited for women, except I'm not allowed to say that, either, since the expression "lady" fell out of favor. Let's just concede that women, by choice, didn't do it much.

The idea of hunkering came about because Beer Bellies Galore, the highly acclaimed Rhode Island rock band, had a gig in Hunker, Pennsylvania, according to the Internet. Such a find—that an entire town is named after a once-common social skill—naturally inspires a practicing pundit, and so I had at it.

Hunkering is a physical position in which one squats on

his—here's that word—haunches. It's a fundamental resting position for man—in fact, for all bipeds, such as chimps, who hunker daily—and has been since we first stood upright. Anthropologists are certain ancient man hunkered at the mouth of his cave to watch a primeval world in about the same way farmers now hunker at the end of a corn row to study the plowed earth.

"Hunker" is a word that comes down to us from the Old Norse terms, *hokra* or *huka*, both meaning "to crouch." The definition is "to squat close to the ground with the body leaning slightly forward, the weight resting on the calves." In English, we've transliterated the word into several forms— "hunky-dory" for "ok," "hunks" meaning "miserly" in early England. "Hunkers" was a synonym for "haunches." In 1845, a "Hunker" was a conservative Democrat in New York State. And of course "hunk" today is a noun, and another thing you can't say about women with any positive result.

There are two essential hunkering styles. In Asia, for example, hunkerers tend to favor the full squat—feet close together, haunches balanced delicately as a center of gravity, arms crossed and resting lightly on the knees. I once saw several men in full squat awaiting a bus beside a rural Tunisian highway but cannot say with certainty all North Africans employ full-squat hunkering. Australians hunker as we do.

In the West, a half-squat style has developed. The Nobel laureate, author John Steinbeck, in his seminal work, *The Grapes of Wrath,* perfectly describes the western hunker: "One foot was flat to the ground, the other rested on the ball and slightly back, so that one knee was higher than the other. Left forearm rested on the lower, left knee; the right elbow on the right knee, and the right fist cupped for the chin. . . ." In western hunkering, the haunches are raised slightly for balance. Chin-holding is optional, but could indicate a timorous quality in the hunkerer.

The act of hunkering in rural America became much more than a resting position, and had both social and business implications. For one thing, hunkering is a classless position, setting all men on equal levels. And it is a non-combative, non-threatening position. You never had anything to fear from a hunkered man.

Out in the country, when families visited on summer Sunday afternoon, the women would gather on the porch in chairs, and the men would congregate in the yard, most of them hunkering and gossiping. If a cattleman was bargaining a sale from a rancher, they might meet by the corral fence, then hunker down during negotiations. It wasn't necessary, but most often the hunkerers kept their hands busy. One might be holding and chewing on a Johnson grass stem or with a small stick drawing patterns in the dirt. Another might whittle on an elm stick while he talked.

For rural folks, hunkering was a natural, comfortable resting position. Hunkering is not a dead pastime, but we have become an urban society where visiting and business are done indoors where there are chairs for sitting. Hunkering is an outdoor activity. I'm sure there are people who live out in the country hunkering right now, but about the only hunkerers I see anymore are cowboys at rodeos who come into the arena to watch the events up close. They hunker down beside the fence to be as inconspicuous as possible to the animals and riders.

They've told me I have to add a disclaimer at this point. No, women did not hunker much, if at all. It simply was not a feminine position, and any women who hunkered would not have been considered a lady. Yes, back then, women wanted to be ladies. But women absolutely are capable of hunkering, no question about that. No one can get by me saying a woman is an inferior hunkerer. A woman can hunker just as well as any man if she wants to. And she certainly has individual choice in the matter. Do it or not, it's up to her. Some women, I would guess, probably can hunker better than men. My suggestion is they don't try it in one of those little mini-skirts that hardly cover their haunches.

Mama
Oswald

She was "Mama Oswald" and we were the "boys." Though later she called us "damn" reporters, or worse, when they—always *they*, which sometimes meant we—became an obsession and made her seem a foolish, paranoid old woman.

An extraordinary, complex woman, Marguerite Oswald for almost two decades imposed a grand and often grotesque eminence, an arresting inelegance, on the outer margins of this century's most emotional public experience. She possessed whatever it is within a great actress that claims the rapt attention of an audience, but for Marguerite it was a rancorous essence that finally, at the end of her life, left her lonely and almost alone, and now anonymous. That stage presence, and the absurdity of it, was certified every time she signed her familiar autograph, "Marguerite C. Oswald," with its trailing authenticator, "Mother of Lee Harvey Oswald," like a corporation flaunting its advertising slogan.

"The Mother Monster," was the way Tommy Thompson, who grew up in Fort Worth and went on to become an acclaimed national writer, once described her to me. "Hurricane Mama" and a "harridan bellowing bassoon sobs" were Thompson's assessment of Marguerite in *Celebrity,* his best-selling novel. *Newsweek* examined Mama and came away with the conclusion that she was almost too terrifying to believe. A Pittsburgh man wrote her, "It is quite clear where your son—the wild animal you raised—inherited his faculty for lying." And someone in Fort Worth sent her an anonymous note: "You should have raised your son to be a Christian. . . . (signed) Your neighbor who knows you very well."

"Mama Gimme," we called her. "Mama Oswald" was an ironic title, not an affectionate one, among local reporters who contended with her for most of the seventeen years she lived after John Kennedy's 1963 assassination.

"Mama called again," a reporter would say, almost sighing.

"What does she want now?" another would ask.

One by one, she wore us down, exhausted us, exasperated us, with histrionic demands and telephone tirades and "official" announcements on the scope and progress of her "case," which always proved to be more testimony of the suffering and persecution dumped on her by the unappreciative world of "they" and "we." Mama Oswald believed herself pivotal in the drama of the assassination, though in reality her place was among the footnotes. She never understood but seemed to have seized that flash point of tragedy in Dallas as a deliverance from what must have been a drab and dreary life, for after Dealey Plaza, Marguerite had a career, purpose, and direction. She was historic.

Her voice opulent with the autocratic nuance of posterity, she once described herself: "I'm a mother in history, I'm all over the world." That self-indulgent divinity—*A Mother in History*—became the title of her biography in 1966 by New

York author Jean Stafford. It is a thin little book in which Marguerite's own words and the ingenuous shrillness with which she spoke them for the astounded author reveal Lee Harvey Oswald's Mother as shrewish and dotty, living in the nether world of "conspiracies" and "lies" and "errors of omission," alternately exalting her assumed historic aristocracy while weeping that she is "oppressed" and "persecuted" and, worse, "abandoned."

"If you research the life of Jesus Christ," lectured Mama, "you find you never did hear anything more about the mother of Jesus after he was crucified."

Mama reasoned: "I think any man in America would be proud to have a mother like me."

Stafford characterized Marguerite as the kind of woman who "treads on your foot in the bus and turns to berate you for it." Loudly.

She was fifty-six in 1963, white hair pulled tightly into a bun, a widow's knot, her round body—"tubular" and "barrel construction" and "frumpish" were common, unflattering descriptions—encased in a rigid girdle, the mouth resolutely dour, her face jowly, creased with what one writer called "iron wrinkles." William Manchester in his authorized assassination history writes of "her heavy jaw, knotted neck muscles, and face the colour of burnished pewter."

Soon after news accounts that a suspect in the JFK assassination, Lee Harvey Oswald, was in custody, Marguerite, with neither friends nor automobile, telephoned the *Star-Telegram* to announce—she never timidly asked for any favor—that she required transportation to Dallas. Editors sent Bob Schieffer as escort/chauffeur/interviewer. She still wore her white nylon nurse's uniform, carried a blue overnight bag and large purse, and, understandably distraught, wept all the way to Dallas, uttering the first of an immeasurable inventory of lamentations: "They all turned their backs on me before [when Lee defected to the Soviet Union in 1959], and they will turn their backs on me again," she wailed as they arrived at the Dallas police station.

Later, Schieffer (now a CBS-TV national correspondent) delivered Marguerite to the Irving home of Lee and wife Marina's friend, Ruth Paine, where that Friday night Thompson became the second reporter to encounter Mama Oswald. Thompson, who died in 1982, tried to speak with Marina, and Mama yelled at him: "Don't you think I should answer that question? I'm his Mother!"

Thompson wrote that she shrieked at Marina: "Whore! You Russian whore! You got my boy and me into this!" She then flung at him a theme that she would echo for a decade—usually citing her "very unusual extrasensory perception": "My boy didn't kill anybody! I'm his *Mother!* And a *Mother* knows!"

Thompson hid the two women in an Adolphus Hotel suite in Dallas, registering as "Sam Swartz and family, Chicago," while finishing his story for *Life* magazine. All too soon, FBI agents found the suite and took the women. Marina and Marguerite were secreted in the manager's apartment of Arlington's Inn of the Six Flags, the site of an "injustice" Mama would bitterly recount for the rest of her life. For Lee's funeral, agents bought Marina a new dress, "but none for me and I am his *Mother!*"

On a late gray Monday afternoon at Rose Hill Cemetery in Fort Worth, Lee was buried in a No. 31 Pine Bluff casket for what almost was a parody of a $710 funeral. Services were delayed three hours because no minister would officiate. Finally, Louis Saunders, who headed Fort Worth's ministerial association, agreed to do it. He had no Bible, spoke only the briefest of eulogies—". . . may God have mercy on his soul"—and told the gathered family members, FBI agents, police, and newsmen, the only audience, that "His Mother has asked me to say that Lee was a good son. . . ." Reporters carried Oswald to his grave. That day Mama did not cry.

The FBI kept Marina but released Marguerite, and she returned to her rented apartment at 2220 Thomas Place in west Fort Worth to prepare for her new role, that of self-ordained *Mother in History,* a characterization for which her maternal sackcloth was patterned with martyrdom and fringed by paranoia.

On December 6, she re-emerged to preside over her first news conference, during which an anonymous caller threatened to shoot her. Police guarded Mama closely. She issued her "official" statement, then began talking. And talking. And talking. And talking. Her voice—with its New Orleans accent—was firm and full, strident and shrill, scolding, imploring, peevish and complaining, indignant, unending. A reporter wrote "Blah" on his note pad.

Reporters were to learn that within Mama's imperative statements were little but words that began with calmness and twisted slowly into a litany of personal agonies and implausible ideas. Pausing only to breathe, she spoke volumes in a voice that flowed with the force of a storm tide, rising, falling, arrhythmic, leaping subjects in mid-sentence, with cadence fitful and aberrant, syntax disheveled and labyrinthine, stressed with exclamation points and underlined boldface italics. Mama's voice, said *Newsweek,* was "a bludgeon, syllable after syllable thudding like blows on the listener's ears."

Fewer and fewer reporters attended her "press conferences" but Mama had placed herself in the eminent domain, like a national park that required attention and regular tending. She put journalists under siege by telephone and letter and telegram, beseeching them to "tell the truth" and give "support" to her "investigation, " her "case," her "documentation," haughtily declaring "I want as much recognition as the Kennedys and Johnsons have had," and "If I solve this case, it will be a one-woman crusade." She promised to continue "my fight for *justice* and our *American way of life*," censuring us, often with profanity and even vulgarity, for our blindness. "The answer to this thing is right in front of you boys, and you can't even see it," she once declared. In those one-sided conversations, she spewed out remarkable revelations about Lee—he was "coming out in history as a very fine person"—and preposterous, even bizarre, ideas on the assassination.

She wanted an American flag for Lee's grave; he was a veteran and "deserved it." She asked that Lee be disinterred and reburied in Arlington National Cemetery, where John Kennedy lay, because "my son is an unsung hero." She requested that her letters and personal belongings along with those of Lee be placed in Boston's John F. Kennedy Library: "They made money by exploiting Lee and accusing him of assassinating Kennedy. My son has become part of history. He should take his place alongside the man they say he murdered."

"So maybe Lee . . . was the assassin," she once said in a moment of concession, "but does that make him a louse. No, no! Killing does not necessarily mean badness. You find killing in some very fine homes for one reason or another."

Hanging on her living room wall was a brass scroll, announcing, "My son—Lee Harvey Oswald—even after his death has done more for his country than any other living human being. . . . (signed) Marguerite C. Oswald."

Mama's earliest, and most outrageous, assassination theory centered on JFK's rumored pending death from Addison's disease, an illness caused by failure of the adrenal glands. She asserted that "he had a lingering disease, [America] couldn't have a lingering president."

"President Kennedy was a dying man," she told Stafford for her biography (and later *Esquire* magazine), "so I can say it is possible that my son was chosen to shoot him in a mercy killing for the security of the country, and if this is true, it was a fine thing to do and my son is a hero. . . . Why wouldn't it be just a normal thing to have a mercy killing of the president?"

Marguerite Oswald was condemned forever by Mama Oswald's words and ideas.

There was about Mama Oswald a harsh, ill-bred brusqueness, an immoderate directness, and she rarely opened a conversation with any but the thinnest veneer of social polish. If she wanted something, she asked for it, and having gotten it or the promise of it, she left with her gratitude intact and ungiven; if denied, she would slam the receiver, often with a departing curse.

It was ungraciousness and seeming greed that painted Mama with the harshest brush. Aside from attention and recognition, what she wanted most was money. She was a woman, decided *Newsweek*, "so errantly mercenary that she honestly cannot understand why, as the Mother of the murderer of the president, she would have to worry about money."

That indeed appeared to be her philosophy, explained in another conversation: "I need the money to carry on the campaign against the campaign against me, and as a mother, I think I deserve it."

Hardly had she shouted her first declaration of motherhood at Tommy Thompson when she announced that *Life* would have to pay her $2,500—"She wanted *quid* for her *quo*," he wrote later. Mama admonished Thompson with what would become a familiar caveat: "I hold all the cards." He refused to pay her, as did later the *Star-Telegram,* other newspapers, and the Associated Press, although she asked often for payment, usually $50 for a quick interview.

On the assassination's tenth anniversary, a UPI reporter, Preston McGraw [one of the seven newsmen who served as pallbearers for Lee at his funeral], telephoned Mama, and she responded: "If you want to pay for my knowledge, fine. If not, go to hell!" Slam, hang up.

JFK's assassination directly affected four women: Jackie, Marina, Mrs. J. D. Tippit, widow of the Dallas police officer shot by Lee, and Mama Oswald. Jackie received the world's sympathy and later married one of its richest men. In 1963, speaking almost no English, pitiable, waiflike, Marina was given perhaps $100,000 in public donations, more money from the sale of Lee's assassination effects to the government, royalties from a book. More than half a million dollars came as gifts for Mrs. Tippit, who remarried and left the public eye.

Mama received $44 in donations, 400 letters—most containing brutally cruel criticism of her—and later $863 from National Life and Accident Insurance Company for a 1945 policy she held on Lee. Nothing more, except seventeen years of living with that day.

Attempting to raise money in March 1964, Mama went public in Chicago with a proposition. Send her money for a secretary, investigators, and living expenses, and in a year, she promised, there would be proof to solve the assassination mystery. Mama got nothing, not a cent.

In 1969, Marguerite found an accommodating attorney and filed suits totaling $25 million, suing everyone she believed had wronged her—writers Jimmy Breslin, Jim Bishop and Manchester, *Look* and *New York* magazines, *Reader's Digest*, U.S. Representative Gerald Ford of Michigan, and CBS. A federal judge dismissed the suits one by one.

With caustic bitterness, Mama assessed her position: "Mrs. Kennedy, a very wealthy woman. Mrs. Tippit, a very wealthy woman. Marina, very wealthy, but I am wondering where my next meal is coming from. It's sometime almost like a spiritual. [Here] we are, we four women in history, and yet I am the Mother. But has anyone come forward to reimburse me for my emotional stability? No, no! And I have given of my time and my voice. [Isn't] it strange? Here is Mrs. Oswald, talking and talking about the American way of life, and where is the rent money coming from?"

To exist, Marguerite demanded and took appearance and interview fees and began selling the only valuable property she possessed—Lee's letters and childhood articles. She got $100 for speaking in New York's Town Hall and $200 for a Los Angeles TV talk show. Anyone who paid Mama to speak got his money's worth. Stafford's publisher paid $1,000 for her biographical interview, marking the check "royalties." For another thousand, *Life* bought a photograph of Mama and Marina together. She made a few dollars by reading Lee's letters for a long-playing album, which sold poorly. She charged the British Broadcasting Corporation $400 for half an hour of her time. For $4,000, *Esquire* purchased and printed sixteen of Lee's letters from the Soviet Union.

Mama auctioned more letters and Oswald papers, including Lee's baptismal certificate through a New York company, Charles Hamilton Autographs Inc. Tucked into a Day-Glo pink catalog beside personal signed messages from Albert Einstein, Ben Franklin, and Mahatma Gandhi, the letter sent from a future assassin, from an errant son to his mother in Fort Worth, Texas, sold for more than $10,000.

Because of Mama's apparent blatant greed and the earnestness with which she disposed of her son's effects, writers called her a "ghoul." *Texas Monthly* wrote, "She is as briskly businesslike about her son's belongings as a medieval monk selling pieces of the true cross."

Criticism failed, for as Mama blithely explained to *Esquire* in 1973 (after collecting $750 for the interview), "If I am going to sign my name I am going to get $100 for it to buy some groceries. I also refuse to let anyone record my voice or take my picture without paying . . . everything in my house, even an ashtray, is a historical item, and it will cost anybody to get one. I would also like to sell the headstone from Lee's grave, but I hope it will go to a museum or library. They know they're not going to get it for nothing."

With the money, which was very little when spread over seventeen years, Mama bought a sky-blue Buick and a small red brick home and grew increasingly rancorous because everybody in the "case" had a book, but not her. She desperately wanted to write a book, as though the fantasy of Historic Mother would somehow become real, immortal, between hard covers. She spoke of "my book" at her first news conference and through the years begged reporters to help her find publishers, implored writers to co-author her manuscript, trailed after lawyers with promised book contracts in their pockets, all without success.

"Robert [her second son] had his book, and Marina . . .," Mama complained in 1977. "I have a story to tell. I don't want to appear that I'm pushing for a book, but after all I am the Mother of the man accused of killing the president of the

United States. After fourteen years of suppression and distortions, I'm proud to have survived—I do not feel sorry for myself. I just can't understand why I don't have a book."

Whenever glutted with paranoia by "them," Mama turned her fantasy writing into a weapon of vengeance: "They are all scum. 'They' framed him good, but I'll fix 'them' in my book!"

She broke into print in the low-rent district, "writing" a three-part series for *National Insider*, a lurid supermarket tabloid. Hidden among the truss ads ("Rupture Agony Cured!") and astrological secrets from Madame Zeus and blood-red headlines about Air Force sex clubs and ministers' wives moonlighting as prostitutes, Marguerite finally told her story. She was paid $60.

Mama's only legacy to the world of letters is a thin publication—mostly *Star-Telegram* funeral photographs, a few acrid memories told with tumbling syntax—carrying the unwieldy title *Aftermath of an Assassination: The Burial and Final Rites of Lee Harvey Oswald as Told by his Mother*. The publisher, Challenge Press of Dallas, felt obliged to offer a disclaimer that it did not intend "in any way [to] impugn the findings of the Warren Commission." *Aftermath* is only sort of a book, not nearly what Mama had in mind as an author, but it is all she left of herself.

She was born Marguerite Claverie in the New Orleans of 1907 to a family of French and German ancestry. The mother died soon after, leaving Marguerite and five siblings in the care of the father, a streetcar conductor. The family never rose from poverty. At seventeen, she quit high school after one year to become a law office receptionist and in August 1929 married Edward John Pic, a clerk, to begin an adult life wrought with little but misery and travail.

Mama's new husband left in her seventh month of pregnancy, and she bore her first son, John Edward, alone. She remarried, this time to Robert E. Lee Oswald, and the second son, Robert, was born. In 1939, again with Marguerite seven months pregnant, the Oswald husband died. Heart attack. Lee was born October 18. After six years, Marguerite tried marriage for the third and last time. An engineer, Edwin A. Ekdahl. The family moved to Benbrook, west of Fort Worth.

Three years later, Ekdahl sued Marguerite for divorce and in an acrimonious jury trial charged that Mama "threw objects at him" and "nagged . . . [and] ranted at him." The jury quickly granted a divorce. Marguerite moved out with her sons, reclaimed the Oswald name and for the rest of her life proclaimed herself a "widow," ignoring the Ekdahl marriage and divorce.

In Fort Worth, this truly dysfunctional family was poor, moving like Bedouins every few months, living on what little Mama earned as a nurse. One by one, her sons dropped out of school and went away to the Marines, where boot camps at Parris Island, South Carolina, may have seemed restful. Her sons never really came home again, and years later the surviving boys told of their disconnection from Mother in Warren Commission testimony.

"I have no motherly love for her," said John Edward, adding, "I think anything he [Lee] may have done was aided with a little extra push from his mother." Understating, Robert said, "She is rather persistent. . . . We have never gotten along." In a later interview, he remembered that "we were a burden to her."

For thirteen months before JFK's murder, Mama did not know where Lee was, nor is there evidence that she even looked for him. John Edward refused all contact with her. She was estranged from her brothers and sisters. Marina would not speak with her nor allow her contact with her granddaughters. For the more than seventeen years after Lee's funeral until her death, she never heard from Robert, who was living in Wichita Falls.

Marguerite, too, testified before the Warren Commission. "A monologue," Earl Warren said. "Hearsay, conjecture and her own opinions." Another commission member said of Mama, "She shows the same kind of persecution complex he [Lee] is supposed to have had. She has the same feelings that people are against her and she tells again and again about unfair treatment she has received."

Nonplused, Mama, dressed in funereal black, staged a news conference and ranted that Marina had been feted in Washington, D.C., but that she had not. Within months Marguerite expressed doubts that commission members would reach a just decision because she had not been "called . . . for counsel in their inquiry."

In late September 1964, one day after release of the Warren Commission summary naming Lee as the lone assassin, I drove Marguerite to her son's grave in Rose Hill Cemetery. It was a warm afternoon, with a bright sun, and it was breezy. She brought fresh flowers, pink mums and white glads. She wore a black dress.

There were, as there always were in the early days, visitors. An old man in a faded Ford who came, walked the few steps to the grave, studied it, and then, before leaving, nodded to Mama, who smiled. Teenagers, shy and hesitant, with a quick glance at the stone, then gone, but not before one boy snatched a few souvenir blades of grass when Mama turned away. A family, five in number, who photographed themselves around the grave. Mama didn't seem to mind.

A tree stood beside the stone, west of it. She never knew who planted it, but the tree, a weeping willow, seemed symbolic, she thought. The grass was extraordinarily green, even in winter. Golf-course grass, she called it. Mama had planted the special grass, on her hands and knees had clipped and trimmed it, and had pruned the tree, because she wanted the grave "nice for the many people who come to take pictures."

She placed the flowers around the headstone. We went home and sat in her study, where a print of WHISTLER'S MOTHER, her favorite painting, hung on the wall. Mama put on her news conference face, summoned her indignity, declaring of the summary: "Marguerite Oswald calls this report a cover-up. The report reeks of politics and the Mother of Lee Harvey Oswald believes it to be a cover-up on many points." And then she wept, more intensely, longer, than I had heard her cry before or ever would again. She said, finally, "It makes me look like a bad mother—I did the best I could."

When I left, she was still crying.

The years passed, and Marguerite finally would not speak to other reporters or me, perhaps believing we had been some kind of penitence for her martyrdom. She closed us out with a final, ringing crescendo of Mamaism, haranguing a reporter: "To hell with you and the radio, and the newspapers, and television and magazines." She continued to "investigate" this crime of the century, now and then declaring her secrets—"I know who pinned Lee" and "I know who framed my son and he knows I know." She promised her files would solve the murder, the conspiracy, but they did not.

After her death, thirty boxes and 480 books were placed in the Texas Christian University library archives, but except for the odd presence of curious bookmarks, such as empty U.S. State Department envelopes, and her acid margin notes—"Wrong!" and "Frame!" and "Is the author sick?

Baloney!" most initialed "MC" because Mama knew her place in history—Mama's investigation files are a fantasy, much as her life.

Mama never stopped searching for the phantom book, perhaps seeing it as an emancipator of her bondage to poverty and loneliness, crying after a decade, "I want to go away . . . to write my book . . . I want to be free. I'm alive. I'd like to get out. I'm stuck here with no money and no friends. My life's not over. I'd like to disappear. Ten years have gone out of my life. I need to be taken out to dinner and dance. I'm not dead yet. I'm only sixty-six . . . I could get away and be free."

Mama was a disagreeable and unlikable woman, unpleasant and difficult to deal with, and she created almost all of her own unhappiness and the disapproval she spread. But Mama was tough and tenacious, persistent, doggedly consistent, a survivor—"I am the strongest person in this tragedy, because I have lost everything," she once said. "Marguerite Oswald has survived."

Look at her without the Mama persona, the hysterical outbursts and effluvium of words, and her demands, her assertions of "truth" had reason in them. With indisputable logic, she insisted that we assign "accused" or "alleged" to Lee's role as assassin because "My boy never received his constitutional right of trial by jury."

JFK's assassination, she finally concluded, was a conspiracy by "high officials" and "important people," the Mafia, CIA, FBI, and "secret agents," of which Lee was one—a theory common around the world. She charged for interviews because, as she explained to one writer, "You're being paid to do the story. Your outfit will make money. What about me?"

Mama sold Lee's things, hawked herself, her "knowledge," like a carnival barker, because she had few other choices. "Do you think I like creating this kind of image for myself?" she once asked in a calm moment. "I know this sounds bad, but I have no other way to live. Is that bad?" She never worked again. She claimed not to have left her house for a two-year period. She said she went more than a year without meat, that she drank Sego evaporated milk, five cans for a dollar. She had $101.60 monthly Social Security, later raised to $191. She was alone for almost two decades.

After November 1963, Lee was dead. Jack Ruby was a piteous, sordid little man. Jackie was beyond approach; Marina went into seclusion. There were no heroes, and few villains, almost no visible surviving characters in the tragedy, but there was Mama Oswald, crass, loud, shrewish, profanely greedy, the pudgy, frumpish burlesque of a mother, pushing her way onto the stage. She wasn't much, but she was all we had.

"I did the best I could," she said while sobbing uncontrollably that long-ago September afternoon, and the simple truth is, Marguerite, who had no mother to teach her the more gentle, merciful ways of mothering, probably did.

I saw her last at a service station in west Fort Worth, waiting for her car to be repaired. "Hello, Mrs. Oswald," I said. She glared at me, turned her back, and did not speak.

She died January 19, 1981, a Saturday, at 5:45 A.M.. in Harris Hospital. Cancer. She was seventy-three. There were few visitors in the hospital or at home. In her final years, C. A. Monismith, a *Star-Telegram* writer, befriended her. He took her to eat in restaurants or on weekend picnics in the park, although Mama-like, she always demanded that she choose the food, probably because paranoia raged within her loneliness. She had a police dog, Fritz, for protection. At one point she was afraid to eat at home. She had some food tested for poison in a local lab.

She had almost no friends, but there were indications she tried to find them. "The neighbors don't even invite me in for coffee, even though I've had them in my house," she told reporter Martha Hand in a lengthy, unpaid, *Star-Telegram* interview. "I have suffered much," she concluded. Mama even reconstituted old grievances: "The *Star-Telegram* owes me. They helped kill my son. They owe me something. They have no right to call him assassin."

In November 1963 there had been a man in her life, perhaps a romantic friend, perhaps not. "Mr. G" he was called. But after the assassination, he wrote her only under an assumed name and with a false return address, and finally he wrote no more. Mama did not speak with her sons or Marina. "I called them, several times," she said, "but they either wouldn't talk to me, or hung up. I don't really give a damn. This is just what I've gone through."

She had another friend, a woman, who patiently waited until Mama accepted her. "It was almost two years before she would allow me to cook food at home and bring it to her." The woman bought special shoes for Marguerite because she had painful arthritis. Mama came to the woman's home, to rest, to sing ("Marguerite had a beautiful voice"), and she read her poetry aloud. In was, inevitably, sad poetry. The friendship was based on a simple premise, the woman said: "I let her talk."

The burial was Sunday, January 20, in Rose Hill. Only five people, including her son, Robert, and a minister, were present. I watched from a distance. The services were brief. She now lies near Lee, but the grave is unmarked at the request of Robert.

The tree is gone. Someone has removed it, or it died. And Bermuda grass, which turns gray and brittle in the winter, overcame the golf-course grass long ago.

For the funeral, there was a spray of pink and white carnations with silver letters spelling out Marguerite Oswald's lasting and only epitaph: Mother.

News You Can
Use and Use
And Use. . . .

Some of this is out-and-out plagiarism, taken from old notes I made long years ago. I've forgotten the source and have lost interest in finding it. I'm stealing the stuff, and that's that. If the author shows up later, he can have it back.

It's about newspapers because I heard again this week that newspapers have no future, that TV and computers will provide all the news we need. This was said by one of those stoop-shouldered young men who wear glasses and blink a lot and think of paper as dead trees. My position is that newspapers will survive because, if nothing else, TV news doesn't have crossword puzzles and Dilbert. You can't clip coupons from computers.

Television news is like those little Velveeta and liver-dabbed canapes you get at cheap weddings. Here we serve up meat and potatoes, with a good peach cobbler for dessert. You watch TV news and think, "That can't be true!" Next morning you read the newspaper to confirm that not only is it true but worse than you ever believed possible. Newspapers are a TV litmus test.

There's nothing else like newspapers. For less than four bits daily, a newspaper is delivered to your house long before dawn. It tells you all the silly and sensational and salutary things people and institutions did the day before, plus noting movie starting times, ballgame scores, births, deaths, bean recipes, and opinions to snort over. A newspaper tells you the day, month, and year. That's valuable information.

The *Star-Telegram's* main news takes about two cups of coffee to get through—then it really becomes useful because what this newspaper actually is, is a handy, all-purpose household tool. I shouldn't reveal our secrets but we use special absorbent paper to help on housekeeping jobs like cleaning windows. Probably you've been putting off the windows because you had to go buy that blue spray stuff and expensive paper towels. We've solved those problems.

Here's what you do: mix a little tap water with household ammonia. Tear off a sheet of, say, the sports section, wad it up, then fluff it a little to give it body. Spray the dirty window and rub. See? The *Star-Telegram* sops up that dirt and water and shines the glass. Best of all, it doesn't leave those little bitty specks like paper towels do. And it doesn't streak. I'm proud to say that we [here at the *Star-Telegram*] like working for a no-streak newspaper that sops up water.

Once you understand how helpful a freshly read newspaper can be, all kinds of uses come to mind. It will serve to empty the vacuum cleaner bag on, line a shelf, train a puppy on, and wrap around fine crystal goblets if you're moving. Shredded, it can be confetti for a party or excelsior to line a box for a cat to have kittens in. It can be cut into paper dolls, folded into hats and boats. When I was young, we made kites using a newspaper page held onto two crossed sticks by flour-based paste and tied pieces of old sheets for a tail. At Christmas, we cut strips, pasted the ends together, and made long chains for tree decorations. We also used the newspaper—the *Star-Telegram,* as it were—to roll crushed cedar bark into homemade cigarettes for smoking behind the barn.

Torn to bits, soaked and mixed with paste, newspaper becomes papier-mâché from which unattractive vases, bowls, and ashtrays are made. You can tack a folded newspaper over a broken windowpane until the repairman comes or hold one over your head in a sudden rainstorm. There's a gadget with which to tightly roll newspapers into serviceable fireplace logs. With real logs, a newspaper can start a blaze quicker and more safely than that liquid fossil fuel. Newspapers can be stuffed under a door crack to keep out cold winter winds or, folded just right, serve as a fan on hot summer days.

I ordered fish and chips from a sidewalk vendor in London, and they were served in a cone of newspaper, as were the fried crab bits I ate at a Tokyo amusement park and the fresh cherries I bought in Salzburg, Austria. In Bombay, my hotel laundry was returned wrapped in newspaper.

Whatever you're doing that's messy—wallpapering or painting, for example—newspapers are perfect for splattering on. It's likely that the most-used recommendation in the English language is "Before you begin, spread a newspaper on the floor."

Sure, you can read, then stack up newspapers for later recycling, but that's the least of their value. In this age of obsolescence, when products are manufactured to be consumed, used up, or worn out quickly, a newspaper is, as that computer kid would say, premium multi-tasking software.

Because this is football season and tailgate parties are in progress, I'll tell you one final *Star-Telegram* secret. You know the routine. You and your friends are all standing around that big old wagon, eating cold fried chicken legs and barbecued ribs and those baked beans with little bacon pieces in them. That's real eating. But it's a messy meal. Here's what you do: take two or three of those fat *Star-Telegram* sections, open and spread them on the tailgate. There you are. No chicken grease or bean juice to stain your paint job. Plus, there's a bonus. Those color photographs we publish can harmonize with the taco salad or avocado dip.

We haven't let it out, but we design spread-open sections of the newspaper to exactly fit the tailgates of the eleven best-selling foreign and domestic family wagons built after 1983. We here at the *Star-Telegram* like having a newspaper that form-fits tailgates and is color-coordinated with plastic salad bowls. This last idea was given to me by an elderly woman who likes stadium parking-lot parties and claims she's been reading and using the *Star-Telegram* for more than sixty years as a handy, all-purpose household tool. She knows how to fry chicken legs just right, and there's no grease on her tailgate.

"Pee-Can?"
That's
Nuts

I don't mind but he always does this: shows up at the wrong time and unexpectedly, with little warning, on his way through from Chicago to Houston, arriving in mid-morning, leaving in late afternoon. I stop everything and feed him Tex-Mex at Joe T's, then tour-guide him around town, though after all these years he's seen and done everything twice except the pecan tree, which he's never visited but mispronounces anyway.

When I mention it, he says, "Pee-can tree?"

"No," I reply. "Puh-kon. Puh . . . puh . . . puh. The 'P' and the 'E' are pronounced 'Puh.' 'C-A-N' is like 'kon'."

"P-E-C-A-N is," he insists, "is 'Pee-can'."

"Puh . . . puh . . . puh," I say. "Kon . . . kon. Puh-kon."

"We're going to see the world's biggest pee-can tree," he told the teenage gas-station cashier, who began working out an answer for whatever she believed he said to her.

"Puh-kon," I translated.

"Oh . . . OH!" she said, relieved.

"Not the world's largest, just in Texas."

"I love pee-cans," he said, and off we went, headed west to Weatherford and Texas' largest puh-kon tree. He was excited.

Out on I-20 West, he asked, "How much farther to the pee-can tree?" If they're going to come down here, the least they can do is learn the language. I don't expect fluency, but they could master a few common terms and phrases, could pronounce our cultural symbols correctly. The puh-kon, after all, is our state tree and nut.

To make my point I told him about the dictionary entry for pecan. Clearly "puh-kon" is the recommended first pronunciation. There's almost equal acceptance for "peh-kon," but that's just the academicians who drafted the dictionary playing with their educations. In their ivory towered pedagese, they lean toward the haughty "peh-kon," but when they talk, they say "puh-kon." Heritage will out, especially in the colorful lingua franca that drives the Texas language.

No question arises over the correct enunciation of the second syllable. Clearly, "can" is said as "kon" because the "a" has two dots over it to indicate an "ah" sound. In the phraseology of those who study such things, these two dots are called, quite casually, "two dots," though there is a German word *umlaut* that means "a change in a vowel sound caused by partial assimilation originally occurring in another syllable, now usually lost."

From that one suspects that p-e-c-a-n earlier had similar spellings, which, of course, it did. "Pacan" is one. That's in the Ojibway tongue. "Pagann," which Crees used, is another. We say "kon" because Indians put an "a" in the first syllable without worrying about the two-dot vowel-correction gambit, which turned out to be still another cultural corruption by the white man.

"My supermarket checker says pee-can. I heard her," he said.

I wanted to educate him on the lore and legends of pecans, of the first papershell Burkett tree found in Callahan County about 1900, of the Jumbo Hollis tree in San Saba that produced pecans so large only thirty-three made a pound; they won a prize at St. Louis' 1904 World Fair, of the WWII memorial tree planted on the Capitol lawn in Austin, nourished by soil from all 254 Texas counties.

I wanted to tell him about the fine practice of "pickin' up pecans" along riverbanks on a crisp fall Saturday afternoon, of thrashing a tree with a cane fishing pole to knock down the ripe pecans—those are the little hard native pecans, but they taste as good as the papershells. I wanted to tell him of "shelling pecans" on a cold winter evening in front of a fireplace, of mixing the pecan halves with butter and salt, baking them until they're dark brown. I wanted him to know how good pecans are in divinity and praline candies and that the only pie in Texas worth eating is a pecan pie made with the state syrup, Karo.

As it was, we got back to the airport, and he was happily telling people that he had his picture taken under Texas largest pee-can tree.

Not really. I've been to Texas' largest pecan tree dozens of time. All you do is turn right on Weatherford's courthouse square and drive north on Texas 51 toward Decatur for 3.6 miles. Down a mild hill, across a narrow creek, and there it is, 200 yards away in the field to your right: ninety feet high, casting a shadow 112 feet wide. Its trunk is twenty feet around.

Except it's been years since I've seen the tree, and other trees have grown up between the master pecan tree and the highway. All that's visible from the road today is the tree's top. I went a little farther and pointed to a tree standing by itself off to my left. "There it is," I said, and he jumped out and took several pictures immediately.

"I want my picture standing under it," he said, handing me the camera, and he jogged across the road, crawled through the barbed wire fence and ran to position himself under the tree for his prize photo. I leaned against a fence post and snapped the shutter.

"Me under Texas' biggest pee-can tree," he gushed, returning to the airport. "I didn't see any pee-cans, though."

"Wrong season," I said.

"Well, that was a big tree."

I thought so, for an elm.

I hope he shows the photo to his supermarket cashier, Chicago's pee-can expert.

Amon's
Will
Be Done

This week, after fifty years of weather wear and tear, the statue was re-unveiled in its bronze splendor. It's sculptress, Electra Waggoner Biggs, now in her eighties and living on the legendary Waggoner Ranch near Vernon, was present to inspect her work of half a century ago titled *Riding into the Sunset,* which is ol' Will slouched on his favorite horse, Soapsuds. Now that ol' Will is cleansed of bird doo and other airborne corrosive pollutants, I'm going to tell this story one last time for posterity and microfilm storage because there should be a public record of it.

The story is about the long boxed-up purgatory of the Will Rogers statue that graces the entrance of the Will Rogers Auditorium/Coliseum complex, Amon Carter, a future president, cops and a lot of money, curiosity and teenagers, one of whom grew up to be the late sweetly eccentric Elston Brooks, for thirty-seven years the *Star-Telegram's* entertainment columnist.

Amon, Rogers' close friend, was so pleased with the statue

that he placed copies at Texas Tech University and the Will Rogers Memorial in Claremore, Oklahoma. He was so pleased with the statue that he waited eight long years to properly introduce it to Fort Worth in a ceremony with General Dwight Eisenhower. President Harry Truman's daughter, Margaret, sang. Bands played. Dignitaries filled the platform. Amon at last had closure of his grief for Rogers, who regularly wandered through Fort Worth because he could be himself here and could, for a little while, not be a public celebrity.

Rogers always said he came to town because he liked the Fort Worth Club's chili. Often after dinner, he would walk across the street to the *Star-Telegram* and visit in its editorial offices, leaning back in a chair, his feet on a desk, talking, talking, talking, interrupting the orderly flow of work. Editors never protested because Rogers was their publisher's friend and because he was entertaining, far more ribald in private than he was in public.

After Rogers' death in Alaska, a distraught Amon needed to memorialize Rogers and caused his name to be placed on the complex being built in west Fort Worth. In 1936, he also commissioned Mrs. Biggs to sculpt a suitable Rogers statue. She gave Rogers an appropriately rumpled look in his early role as a cowboy, which he was, and not the humorist and American icon he had become at his 1935 death by airplane crash in Alaska. There's a simple, very alive spirit to the bronze, and one almost expects Soapsuds—modeled from a New York policeman's horse—to step off the pedestal and lope west toward Amon Carter's museum. Mrs. Biggs completed the work in 1939, but World War II was coming, and Amon couldn't settle on unveiling ceremonies befitting his need for an impressive public commemoration.

He boxed up ol' Will with planking and waited.

And Fort Worth waited, becoming more and more curious about the unseen statue out there on the West Side, so curious that now and then, always at night, someone would rip off several boards for a glimpse of ol' Will. Each time, Amon grumbled and fussed, then boxed up the statue again.

In mid-1947, Elston Brooks was a Paschal High School senior, and in that summer the statue was unboarded twice in one week. Amon's friends at the Fort Worth Club pulled off the first midnight raid. They had been drinking a little. Later in the week, Brooks and several other teenagers arrived at the newly planked statue shortly before midnight. Not very artfully, they ripped off all of ol' Will's fresh planks and gawked at the ten-foot-tall, 3,000-pound statue. For Amon, that was the last plank.

By 9 a.m. the next morning, he was offering a $5,000 reward for capture and successful prosecution of the statue raiders. Before his death, Elston recalled that the reward assured that he and his friends would be caught. He was right.

In those days, policemen could accept rewards, and—a retired cop once remembered for me—all petty crimes in Fort Worth, like murders, rapes, wrecks, and robberies, went wanting for investigation while the police force concentrated on tracking down the statue gang.

Elston's arrest went like this: one teenager bragged to his girlfriend. She told her mother. Mama called the police and immediately demanded the reward. The boyfriend was brought in and gave state's evidence, identifying everyone involved. The teenagers and their parents received a summons to appear at the police station, where they waited in a large interrogation room. In burst an angry Amon Carter, who began lecturing them on the evils of vandalism and juvenile delinquency. He promised them their names would be published in the *Star-Telegram,* breaking a longstanding policy against printing juvenile offenders' names. And, he shouted, he was barring them for life from ever entering the Will Rogers complex buildings. The tirade over, Amon said he would not press charges, and everyone went home. Amon also decided that no one had specific claim on the reward and he donated the money to the Fort Worth Police Benevolence Society.

Ol' Will never again was uncrated, not until official dedication ceremonies later in the year.

After graduation, Elston was hired by the newspaper as a beginning police reporter. He often saw Amon Carter, but neither ever mentioned the statue caper again.

Today, all—Amon, Elston, and a newly bright and shining ol' Will—rest in peace.

O, Say,
Can You
Secede?

My goodness, but that Republic of Texas bunch blew up in all directions, didn't they? I only wish they had checked with me before the fighting started. I tried to secede in 1977 and gave up without firing a shot. We're stuck with America, and that's all there is to it. Now, twenty years later the ROT insurrection fizzled because it overlooked *Roberts Report 700,* the case of *Texas v. White,* and the fact that the rest of us were too tired to join in and mutiny at this time, revolt being a wearying pastime after you've already put in a full eight-hour work day.

So, ignorant and impulsive, what happened to the 1990s ROT? Well, the action-first branch of abundantly armed members abandoned their besieged chic and class-appropriate trailer-house embassy out near Fort Davis, backed themselves into a box canyon, were pursued and captured the way Hoot Gibson used to do it with his cowboy posse. Nobody was hanged, but one ROTer was shot and killed. Before Hoot quit the range, we called that frontier justice. Today it's just a sound bite.

Additionally, from other ROT divisions, a few members were jailed for fraud, bad checks, and such. I haven't studied the matter closely, but ROT seems to have scattered into several camps, each claiming itself the One True Path, all denying any association with the musketeers of Fort Davis, and all suggesting they are no more a public menace than belligerent Rotary clubs.

Or perhaps there's still just one ROT with numerous spokesmen, each hawking a different prescription for Texas secession and freedom to run up a huge national debt on our own—the latter is the reason the original Republic of Texas got us into this predicament in the first place.

After the victory at San Jacinto, after Texas independence was secured, we formed up into a republic. Other nations recognized us, and Texas sent out envoys and ambassadors (a trailer-house embassy is true to the Republic of Texas culture; legend has it our first London embassy was above a popular and convenient bordello).

The government, as governments are inclined to do, was anxious to tax and spend. We printed paper money, but did it on the cheap, leaving one side blank. With nothing to support the currency, value soon fell to nothing.

The problem was Texas had no industry, aside from saloons and a little slave-produced cotton. The only taxable land was what the Republic had given away to new immigrants. The population was small, widely dispersed, self-sustaining, very poor, uneducated, hostile, and suspicious of and highly resistant to any authority, including its own government. (And still is.) The Republic was in trouble.

In 1845, Manifest Destiny came courting. America needed Texas to secure its southwest boundaries, and we negotiated entry into the Union on excellent terms granted no other state. We kept all our public lands, we could at any time split into five states and—here is the loop that 1990s ROT is attempting to slip through—maybe, *and only maybe* (no one has ever been quite sure) we could leave when we wanted.

In 1977, I was in a particularly foul humor over Jimmy Carter's refusal to endorse Billy Beer. Enough was enough. I wrote then-Texas Attorney General John Hill that "I've decided to secede and take Texas with me. Please send all the paperwork."

In due time, an assistant attorney general, Martha Allen, replied that "this office cannot give official opinions to anyone other than individuals enumerated in Article 4399, *Vernon's Texas Civil Statutes,* a copy of which is attached," and it was. I didn't qualify. Ms. Allen, however, had become curious and passed along her research notes on the matter. (That an elected official's office would knowingly break the law restored my faith in the American political system, and I have been faithful ever since; it's good to know that you can still count on tradition in Texas).

Being a lawyer, Ms. Allen couched her answer in legalese, but for those 1990s ROT die-hards, the gist of the message is this: Call in the dogs, and put the chairs in the wagon. The deal's off. Texas can't secede because Texas *already* has seceded. Remember the Civil War? Against all wisdom, God, and Sam Houston, we sided with the South and left the Union, an action that made the 1845 question irrelevant. We went out, legal or not.

Or did we? One theory was that we did and after losing should be treated as conquered territory, like one of those Balkan provinces. Lincoln took the high road, contending that the "United States" was a literal term and, legalities aside, the Union was "indestructible."

We should be proud that the state secession question was

fixed forever because Texas attempted—no surprise here—
a little chicanery with U.S. bonds we held before the Civil
War. We sold them without the governor's signature, and
the U.S. treasury refused to pay, thus a bond purchaser sued
Texas for his money. *Texas v. White* went to the Supreme
Court, and the suit was used to prove the United States had
an "indissoluble relation."

Chief Justice Salmon Chase presented the decision (thoroughly discussed in *A Concise History of the American
Republic*, by Henry Steele Commager, page 725), advised
the meticulous Ms. Allen. She also cited *Wallace Reports
700*, Supreme Court, 1868, and William Whattley Pierson's
Texas v. White, A Study in Legal History, published in 1916
by Seeman Printery, Durman, North Carolina.

The decision began: "The Constitution, in all of its pro-
visions, looks to an indestructible Union, composed of
indestructible States." It went on: "The act which consum-
mated [Texas'] admission into the Union was something
more than a compact; it was the incorporation of a new
member into the political body."

Justice Chase then banged home the clincher on the issue
of state secession rights: "And it was final." That was that.

So, there you are, 1990s ROT. Secession is an extinct
species. Can't be done. If you'll settle for a lesser prize, you
might go the one-into-five route. A few earlier attempts
almost succeeded. One of the first plans was to split Texas
in half and make the Panhandle an Indian reservation, in
which case Lubbock and Amarillo today would be huge
bingo parlors.

Another movement tried to establish The State of West
Texas, even drew up a Constitution and Bill of Rights: "All
political power is inherent in the people." That movement

failed, and West Texas never became an independent state. Did it?

In 1915, a group wanted the Panhandle to be "The State of Jefferson." A piece of East Texas tried to break away in the late 1930s.

Try it if you wish, but know that the one-state advocates have emotion and one unanswerable question on their side. As Guy Bryan, speaking to Veterans of the Texas Revolution in 1873, shouted on the issue: "Texas, Texas! Sound it, think of it. She has but one Lone Star. Every point of that star must remain, for when you take them away the star is gone. Who will put out this glorious luminary? What mercenary, with soul so dead, would barter it away? We plead for the unity of Texas, as Camillus pleaded for one Rome! Divide, and the fragments with their contracted limits, will be common. Texas [as] a unit shall be forever—forever shall be united!"

There is passion for oneness in all forms. Besides, whenever the argument comes up, some Texas patriot always presents the unsolvable puzzle. "Which Texas state," the patriot inevitably asks, "gets possession of the Alamo and Willie Nelson?"

Take my advice. Don't mess around with splitting up Willie.

The Twang's
the Thang,
Ya'll

As cultural tidal changes often do, it's come upon me slow-ly and obliquely that *ya'll* is in trouble, and *ain't* ain't doing too good either, the latter at best a peaked shadowing of itself. I'm fidgety about both. And if ya'll can't pronounce "peaked" right, the situation is worse than I suspect.

The more astute of ya'll will recognize that I used this ubiquitous collective pronoun correctly, meaning it can apply to one person or, say, the entire population of Shanghai, China. I can direct a *ya'll* at a single individual ("Ya'll want that in a roadie cup?") or, alternately, yell to everybody in Shanghai at once, "How ya'll fixed for whip-out?" and count on a group response like "Ging buyao fang weijing, Fugin Clinton" (this means "The check's in the mail, Bill"; the Chinese have a keen sense of humor).

Pronounced as it should be, it's "yawl," slightly drawn-out and nasal, never, ever "you-all" as mis-mumbled by pre-tenders and newcomers to Texanisms or those bad actors in cheap TV movies. *Ya'll* is not a two-syllable word. I spelled it right, as opposed to the form too often written by non-Texans: "y'all."

Having fully explained this necessary Texas word, I will get on with the message that I hear it used less and less these days, and too often without the patented nasal twang required to give it full authority of heritage.

We are losing our Texas brogue, that gravelly *lingua franca* that identifies us, separates us from the rest of the accent-bearing southern states. It's a given fact that aside from Maine and parts of old Brooklyn, the South and Texas produced the only distinctive regional accents. Everywhere else, people talk blandly. For example, except for the curious dietary habit of eating only foods that end in a vowel, Californians are indistinguishable from Michiganders. With our accents fading into a dreary sameness, we may as well live in Iowa where everybody sounds like they went to radio-announcing school.

The Texas accent, particularly for West Texans, came with the territory, blended with the myths and is—was—as obvious as a birthmark. Texans have a mutated gene of rustic rube that long ago was bred out of most Americans. Psychology explains it in terms of "ego-validation" and the "ontological verity of self-invention." Texas writer Larry L. King just called it "playing cowboy."

Others save the heirlooms of their past—the grandmother chiffoniers, the forefather rockers, the ancestral stoneware pitchers. We preserve the character in an acting-out of what was. It comes in exaggerated dress, the boots of exotic animal skins, the wide-brimmed hats, silvered buckles of ordinary businessmen who never rode a horse, a roiling balls-of-feet walk—the John Wayne canter—and measured but emphatic hand gestures, especially in the way we talk.

The speech is a rough prairie patois, opulent in metaphor and simile ("lighter than a June frost"), earthy and often profane, lazy and affable ("boot-broke and hat-happy"), often sexist, even racist, spoken nasally with ungrammatical self-deprecating humor ("I ain't got no dawg under that porch"), calculated to hide any shred of cultural polish and education, echoing of an era in Texas when book-learning was suspicious. Behind all of this, many Texans have hidden well the fact that they have a metaphysical twist of mind and actually read a book now and then. We revel in our Bubba-ness.

No question but our basic accent came from the mid-South region, brought by immigrants who had blended a form of Elizabethan English with ignorance and stirred well. The true southern accent is softer, rounder than ours, and traces of it remain in East Texas. But the true Texas accent begins beyond the 97th parallel, as rough and sharp-edged as the land itself—"It is well-fixed on the Southwestern plains and in cities like Fort Worth and Dallas," linguist W. Cabell Greet once wrote. This is the accent outsiders expect.

The South gave us *ya'll*, not surprisingly contracted from *you-all*, which possibly was used in fourteenth-century England. But the South also said "You-uns" and "we-uns," which we were savvy enough to ignore. H. L. Mencken, in his seminal *The American Language*, footnotes dozens of scholarly studies on *you-all*, including one that proves a similar term appears in Hindustani slang. I suspect *ya'll* arrived in Texas as *you-all*, and we simply squeezed it down to a single workable syllable for economy's sake.

It's our children who are not carrying on the accent, because parents aren't working hard enough on their *ya'lls* and *ain'ts*, and teachers can't be counted on to get far enough away from grammar rules for real learning to take place. So, we are educating our kids' accents away, perhaps as one of those misguided sops to collective self-esteem— the theory that a distinctive, elevating accent might make some other drab-speaking child feel bad about himself. But the truth is, you can't teach every child to say *ain't* and expect it to stick. They have to be raised right.

Television, the babysitter of several generations, is the main slayer of regional accents. It teaches sameness. From toddler age upward, they just sit there absorbing it all. I suppose we should be thankful our kids don't all sound like Kermit the Frog. Probably we should ban all television, except for football games and any movie with Julia Roberts in it, for everyone.

If things get worse, we may have to start up retro-English classes to freshen fading accents, hold anti-enunciation sem-inars to get kids back to droppin' *g's* off words that don't need them. Make them write *ain't* 100 times on the black-board; repetition is the key to learning.

Cleveland Colquitt, Where Are You?

I got lost one fine autumn day down by Votaw when . . . no, wait . . . it was Center Grove because I remember the logging road left FM 942 east of Ollie past that split-fork oak. Or was that Caney Creek? I know I was in Polk County, because I passed Moscow on FM 62, looking for Mr. Colquitt's syrup mill when I found the old house. It happens that way sometimes, in autumn, in deepest East Texas. You lose what you're looking for, only to find something else.

Snuggled onto the western Louisiana line, East Texas has four national forests, and lakes, small towns, and no interstates—only wandering two-lane highways, off which run narrow woodland side roads, a few hot-topped, most unpaved, unnamed, and unnumbered. I was on one of those because my instructions were to "go through Barnes and take the first left where the fence leans." I did and after a few miles the forest squeezed in and the dirt track ended against a creek back of an old house.

Only thin spindles of sunlight filtered through the trees

but the house was dead, its wood rotting and weather-blanched. Inside was dust and a broken table beside a torn box. On the porch was a one-legged rocking chair, its cane seat ripped open, but it would hold my weight and I sat, listening to the extravagant silence.

In East Texas' autumns, the forest smells of genesis, both freshly made and primeval, and the wind whiffles through trees as it might in those lusty Victorian novels for lovers' evening trysts. I watched a turtle on the creek bank, and a redheaded woodpecker that probably was visiting from the Big Thicket, that great swamp-forest bordering on Polk County's southern line, beyond the Alabama-Coushatta Indian reservation.

I didn't care that I had lost the way to Mr. Colquitt's syrup mill, though, without exaggeration, he is one of the world's few remaining independent makers of backyard syrup. Each mid-fall he harvests his sugar cane and then cooks syrup in black kettles perhaps as old as he. People come and stand around, talking and visiting, and buy Mr. Colquitt's syrup—either ribbon cane or sorghum—in quart buckets to take home. It is an experience that may not last out the twentieth century.

It was almost dark when I left the porch and its broken rocker. I found U.S. 287 and drove south to Woodville for dinner at Pickett House because there are few remaining boarding-houses serving handmade family-style meals. Chicken and dumplings is the lure, and butter beans with salt pork, meat loaf, turnip greens, fried okra, hot biscuits, chicken livers and gizzards, watermelon rind preserves, presented in big bowls spread on oilcloth-covered long tables and passed from hand to hand. A family feast.

I mentioned my search for Mr. Colquitt, and the man at the end said my mistake was turning too soon beyond

Barnes, that the proper road was before the old filling station. I thought I might try again. If I didn't find Mr. Colquitt, I would find some other place.

As far as directions to his home, Mr. Colquitt feels that anyone "gettin' left on the hot-top out of Barnes, and come on down, and left again down there" will find his house and syrup mill. Maybe not.

He says he will begin making syrup about the second week of November. And, no, Mr. Colquitt said he didn't know what he would charge for his syrup this fall, but plans to study on it. He promises "a fair price."

Just to get a second opinion, I sought help from the Polk County Chamber of Commerce in Livingston. A spokesperson admitted that finding Cleveland Colquitt is "a little hard" but believed a left on the first "blacktop past Barnes, and maybe the next right" would locate the syrup mill. Maybe not. As the spokesperson pointed out, the Polk County telephone directory listed Mr. Colquitt as a resident of the tiny community of Ruby, not Barnes, but "the telephone company didn't always know what it was talking about."

If you can't find Mr. Colquitt, try a regenerative meal at Pickett House, Texas 190, in Woodville, (409) 283-3371. All you can eat, family style. Open 11 a.m.–2 p.m. Monday/Friday, 11 A.M.–8 P.M..Saturday, and 11 A.M.–6 P.M. Sunday. Adults, said a restaurant spokesman, pay "close to $7, or a little more." Maybe not. When the man at the end of the table passes you the chicken and dumplings, ask him about finding Cleveland Colquitt's syrup mill. That worked one time for me.

Tiptoe
Through the
Pigweed

A Texas drought simply destroys a good lawn and I'm sure that if we don't receive some rain soon my weeds cannot survive. Already my sowthistles are sagging. My woolly croton is woeful. My smut-grass is shabby. My curly dock is critically brownish, starving for moisture. Tend to them as I will, they seem to grow weaker.

It's not an easy matter, this raising of weeds, but I have gone about it systematically and scientifically and am having some modest success. First, I had my soil analyzed to ensure that it lacked fertility. Too much potassium, nitrogen, and iron retards the growth of weeds. My soil, fortunately, is a virtual turf corpse, fit only for bermuda grass and the like.

My basic trouble with the lawn is that I have neglected it. St. Augustine grass took it over. That stuff almost is impossible to get rid of. Once you let St. Augustine get a stand it just grows and grows. Bermuda grass is almost as bad but at least shade will destroy it. At first, the St. Augustine beat me. Sometimes you can drown it, but pouring water on it did not seem to help. I bought several dozen army worms from a nursery and set them loose on the lawn. But the St. Augustine beat them off and continued to thrive.

What really saved my yard was fungus, and I cannot praise it too highly. I consider it an act of God since the fungus just showed up one fine day and began work. That root rot dived right in and began eating up the St. Augustine. By the end of last summer, the grass was gone. I offered to help get fungus started in my neighbors' yard, but they refused. They are strange people.

I worked all winter on my weeds. With the advice of the Texas A&M Agricultural Extension Service I raked leaves and began a compost pile. In beds along the front of the house I planted redroot pigweed, and it is doing nicely, except the lack of rain and city watering restrictions have kept it from reaching its full height of six feet.

Beside the garage I planted a stand of blessed thistle. It burst into flower in February, but the thistle primarily is a winter shrub, and I am thinking of replacing it with hairy galinsoga, which is a hardier plant. In the backyard I have sown camphorweed, dogfennel, sowthistle, purple nutsedge, spotted spurge, goose grass, henbit, prickly side, and for exotic contrast, a small bed of horsenettle. Mostly I have simply planted the weeds in a random fashion since they seem prettier when they are without a forced, rigid pattern. The esthetics are more obvious and natural.

Nothing gives me as much pleasure as sitting on my patio in the late afternoon and watching the sun set over my weeds. I am most proud of my bed of Johnson grass, since the plant takes a sure hand to grow. I planted a bed in the front yard, near the street, for the pleasures of passers-by. Frankly, I've given the Johnson grass more care than the rest of my weeds. It is a highlight of my lawn. The Johnson grass is five feet high now, even without the needed rain, and doing very well. Seeds are almost an inch long and that may be a record. I have written to A&M to find out.

There has been only one problem. A few Johnson grass seeds blew, as seeds will, into a neighbor's yard and fortunately took root. He now has the beginning of a good patch of Johnson grass. He doesn't seem appreciative, though, and actually is trying to kill the Johnson grass. Obviously, he doesn't care about property values, but some people do not like a pretty lawn. As I said he is a strange man and I do not understand him.

The Eyes of Texas
Were upon
Them

It's a little-known fact that Texas' original topless rock 'n roll band first performed in the Metroplex. Mark it down that the musical group's name was the Ladybirds, which makes all the difference in the world when you're talking topless. I was there. Being topless in public was considered sinful sin in the 1960s. Now, as the century comes to an end, we have managed to move partial-nakedness to the ho-hum column.

Dallas, a hotel conference room, was the venue, and the Ladybirds staged a press conference to explain how they were about to get half-naked for their concerts. I suspected a demonstration would occur, and so apparently did the other twenty-seven newspaper reporters, eight radio newsmen, four TV cameramen, several hotel employees on their coffee break, and a guy who had been on his way to a Rotary Club meeting when he stopped to see what the hubbub was all about.

The Ladybirds—who claimed their name was in no way influenced by President Lyndon Johnson's wife, Ladybird; it only was a coincidence—were to play that night at Fort Worth's Casino Ballroom, then return to Dallas for their second engagement. Maybe. What the Ladybirds did was play music to be arrested by. Police in those days did not always find redeeming artistic value in their work.

So there we were, waiting, and the Ladybirds entered. They wore spangled and silvered costumes with big bows in front. Immediately, they dashed off a quick song. I've forgotten what. Then one (named Robin) turned to another (Marcelle) and the following conversation took place:

"I feel funny."

"Me, too."

"It's hot in here," said Robin.

The Ladybirds did an about-face. In unison, there were ten snaps, loud in the now-silent room, like a firing squad sliding back rifle bolts.

Five bows dropped, as did the Rotarian's chin.

The Ladybirds turned to their audience. There in Texas for the first time was an all-girl topless band. A fair assessment is that it was like being barefooted from the waist up.

Then the Ladybirds played and sang again. Let it be recorded that the first song played and sung with half-naked urgency but all sincerity was "The Eyes of Texas." Camera flashes were blinding.

The Ladybirds were three redheads and two blondes who played songs on amplified guitars, one set of drums, and a piano. For practical reasons none of them played the accordion. The music mostly was lots of yeah, yeah, yeah and bass drum beats, neither Mozart nor great art, but it surely passed a rainy afternoon nicely.

The Ladybirds were born of a simple idea in San Francisco, when none of the five 'Birds could play an instrument but decided they could use other assets. At first, practicing in San Francisco, they faked the instruments while a tape recorder provided the notes. Gradually, they learned to play a little, at least enough to be arrested in New York and boycotted in Las Vegas. Counting left to right, they were Barbara, thirty-five, Marcelle, forty, Robin, thirty-six (all on guitars), Rosita, thirty-seven, (drums), and Debbie, thirty-six (piano). Those are not ages. The girls averaged out at 36 4/5 inches, which was not at all average.

Their performing costume was a brief silvered costume with a detachable bow. With the bow off, the costume came dangerously close to being a belt. The Ladybirds were being stared at by reporters and the Rotarian, who were blistering their hands to the best version of "The Eyes of Texas" they had ever heard. Finally, someone got up enough nerve to ask a musical question:

"Aren't those guitars cold?"

"Not very," was the answer.

The ice broken, questions flowed ceaselessly. An exchange with Robin went something like this:

Q. "Didn't you feel, well, funny the first time you performed topless?"

A. "Well, I'm not topless, as you can see. I'm just uncovered. And no, I did not. I know I'm a woman."

Q. "Do you think people come to see you or hear you play?"

A. "The topless thing is an attention getter but I think they may come to see us the first time and come back to hear us play." (A reporter commented sotto voce "Uh-huh.")

Q. "Do you think the topless gimmick will fade with you and the public lose interest, even in your music?"

A. "Well, there are a lot of bands around barely making it."

In retrospect, that's the same way the Ladybirds were making it.

Touchdown
In a Small
Town

When I was young, we played a game called football in West Texas, but by then the sport was almost genteel. For one thing, biting and leg whipping had been outlawed, and that, some said, took away a dependable prospect of bloodiness from the game.

A generation or two earlier, football without broken bones or wounds was considered unmanly. Looking back, football as it was played in the 1930s and 1940s West Texas was a genetic consequence of time and space. It was a rural, agrarian society of isolated communities, and unremittingly male dominated. Half-grown boys needed public certification, and football—someone once explained—was a natural extension to saloon fights common in nineteenth-century Texas.

The necessary skills of football translated easily from the boys' ranching work. Tackling was little different than bulldogging a steer, passing identical to the arm motion of tossing a rope. Players who were "jackrabbit-quick and bullstrengthed" (as one newspaper wrote of its local high school team) could find easy acceptance among the grown men who lounged around their towns each fall when crops were in, cattle auctioned, and time hung heavy in the receding summer heat.

You only have to look at the nicknames given players of that era to understand the masculinity of the game: "Bull," "Big 'un," "Bullet," "Ox." This pedigree of virility was expressed, too, in team names, which in West Texas meant a menagerie of Longhorns and Mustangs, Coyotes and Wolves, even mythical forces like the Dumas Demons and Rankin Red Devils, the Buckaroos of Breckenridge, and the Plowboys of Roscoe. The Mules of Muleshoe and the Blizzards of Winter were natural team names, but how Trent ever decided on Gorillas as the school symbol remains a mystery.

The more temperate world was far away from the West Texas of the Depression years. Out on those hardscrabble plains, distance and loneliness were mean neighbors and any diversion, even a high school sport, relieved the tedium of small towns separated by an autocratic environment. High school football, then, became the measure of a community's stature. The self-esteem of a town rose and fell with the fortunes of its football team, and a municipal won-loss record had the absolute volatility of any urban stock market. Win, and no other environmental force—not sandstorms or drought or searing heat—mattered; lose, and even record-setting high cattle prices couldn't raise morale.

It was almost tribal as a team went out each fall to attack neighboring gridiron squads, often followed by most of the town population. Only the elderly and the infirm stayed behind. By noon of an October Friday when, say, the Munday Moguls left to challenge the Hamlin Pied Pipers, schools would have closed, stores and municipal offices shut down, streets emptied. The team bus would lead a convoy of old flivvers toward the battleground, which often was nothing more than a barren and rocky 100-yard-long rectangle marked by chalk dust on the open prairie.

As a young sportswriter, I remember covering a game at farflung Balmorhea. The field, encircled by a barbed-wire fence, had no grandstands. Fans simply nosed their cars up to the fence, a coin was tossed, the referee blew his whistle, and the teams kicked off. I can't remember who won but there were only two fistfights among spectators, which indicated modest interest in the outcome.

Then World War II came, and rawboned boys went off to prove their manhood in real combat. When they returned, West Texas was almost civilized. By the late 1950s, the cult of West Texas football was almost over, though it was years later before other, gentler, sports were accepted without the caveat of a manhood test.

Once I heard an exchange between two fathers drinking early-morning coffee in a small-town cafe. One asked the other, "Yore boy goin' out for football?"

The second father hesitated, glanced away, then back into his coffee cup and admitted, "Naw, he's gonna play basketball."

Looking pained, the first man blurted, "Gawd amighty, can't you break him of it!"

If You Wish

upon a

Furculum

When seeking current wisdom on poultry parts, one naturally turns to Texas A&M University, which employs Professors of Chickens. The Aggies know farm animals.

"Expediency," explained Dr. Sarah Birkhold, whose title actually is poultry specialist for the university's agriculture extension service. The professor teaches the intricacies of chicken technology and other fowl ideology in A&M's poultry science department. We were discussing the demise of the chicken furculum as a cultural icon, good luck totem, and finest kind of white meat eating part, resulting from my inquiry on one of the more pressing chicken mysteries of the day—that is, whatever happened to the pulley bone? (Or, as most everyone north of Enid, Oklahoma, says: the wishbone.)

Dr. Birkhold, the expert, believes that it, as the rest of us, fell victim to the machine age's rush-to-market frenzy and the Baby Boomers' choice of the shrink-wrapped quartered breast as the best-selling chicken item in the supermarket.

This came about because Colonel Sanders conditioned a generation's chicken-eating habits to quarter-breast pieces. To keep up with demand, chicken plants simply ran carcasses through a sawing machine, and still do. Hand-cutting chickens is expensive labor.

Buzz, buzz. Two directions, and there you have the modern quartered chicken. And a sawed-apart pulley bone—or furculum, as it is known in textbooks—which hangs off the front of a chicken breast and is somewhat analogous to the human collarbone. The pulley bone meat is the chateaubriand of chicken breast and was lusted after for taste alone, but for thousands of years the bone had the mystique of granting wishes or bestowing good fortune.

In my time, fried chicken was the Sunday dinner of choice, and chickens were raised behind the farmhouse. At dawn, my ninety-pound grandmother would select a fat hen, grasp it by the neck, and swing. The hen would make a loop, but the head didn't. Wringing a chicken's neck took practice—like hitting a big league curve ball, it's all in the wrists—but every farm wife could do it.

Inside, a huge pot of water already was boiling. The now-headless, feetless, and gutted hen went into the water for several minutes. This loosened the feathers. My job was to pick off the chicken feathers. Then she cut up the chicken, and the best fat piece was the pulley bone. After church, for Sunday dinner, I got the pulley bone if I had been good that week.

Every morsel of white meat was eaten from the Y-shaped bone. The ritual was that I took one limb of the bone, my grandfather would take the other. We'd make a wish and pull until the bone broke. Whoever got the larger piece would have his wish granted. This wishbone ceremony had changed little since the Etruscans, a fey branch of Italians, began the practice in, said one source, 332 B.C. Etruscans had decided the chicken could forecast the future because every time a hen cackled out popped an egg. So, the chicken became an oracle. Women could choose husbands by allowing a chicken to randomly peck at corn scattered on an alphabet chart. If the chicken first pecked at an "H," for example, then the husband's name would begin with that letter. Afterward, the chicken was killed, the wishbone extracted, and the woman pulled with a friend. If she got the bigger piece, her marriage would be successful.

The Romans believed the Etruscans were strange, but they took on the wishbone habit and carried it to England, where the Brits named this lucky chicken part the "merry thought," though no one seems to know why. The marriage/wish ritual was recorded as early as 1589, and the English were serious about the whole thing. By 1719, in a book called *Omens,* the author writes, "I have seen a man in love grow pale, and lose his appetite upon the plucking of a merry thought."

Imagine the superstitious Pilgrims' delight in the first American Thanksgiving and the discovery of a huge turkey merry thought. (Dr. Birkhold would like you to know that all birds—name one: quail, peacocks, canaries, even the ostrich—have a wishbone; it's in the fowl genes.) The wishbone custom spread everywhere across this country. It even gave us the slang expression: "lucky break."

At one time, the wishbone was a symbol of luck, along with the rabbit's foot, horseshoe, and four-leaf clover. You could buy little gold and silver wishbones for charm bracelets. The wishbone even lent its name to a highly successful football offense, created right here in Fort Worth and spread nationwide. That's curious because we usually say—or said—pulley bone, not wishbone. Yes, social scientists have studied the matter. "Wishbone" mostly is a northern term (except for the far southern tip of Louisiana, where Cajuns say nothing but "wishbone"). One study showed that only twenty percent of Texans between ages fifty and fifty-nine said "wishbone." We're basically "pulley bone" people (favored five to two in Houston, according to a "Forked Bone of a Chicken" linguistics map).

I began searching for a supermarket pulley bone several months ago, but the young meatpersons had no idea what I was asking for. I found finally an older man who said chicken companies once prepared and sold an all-pulley bone package, but no more. The breast-quartering machine arrived.

I e-mailed Tyson, the chicken firm, and asked for an answer to the pulley-bone dilemma. The reply was a little terse (apparently working with dead chickens all day is a stressful job): "We have a Fresh Chicken item (2830) that is a 9-piece cut and includes the pulley bone." My supermarket never heard of it. The anonymous Tyson writer, in a snippy manner, added, "I usually buy a whole chicken and cut it myself."

Sure, that's an answer, but no one can cut up chickens with pulley bones anymore. Once, every housewife could do it. Housewife? Well, that was a woman who stayed home when her husband went off to work and the children to school. Her job was to keep the house clean and neat, cook meals, make sure all errands were run, chores done. She could cut up a chicken. She knew pulley bones. You don't see a lot of housewives anymore. Now, with 2000 upon us, many of the few remaining housewives are, in fact, men, but that's another subject entirely.

A Paradox
In
Pearls

Political correctness has flat ruined my proficiency at grumbling over the muddled and often bizarre conduct of women in general, Texas women in particular. Though they are odd and erratic by nature and training, I'm not allowed to say so anymore because today's women are supposed to be thought of just like men, except for pattern baldness and fly-front underwear.

This is a ironic situation because from the beginning Texas women were as tough, often tougher, and independent as the men. The state's history is rife with stories of women shooting Indians and bad guys, riding on cattle drives, plowing cotton fields. Especially in West Texas, women did what had to be done. They ran ranches, broke wild horses, branded cattle, fought drought and prairie fires. Necessity made the sexes equal, and the West Texas woman was a formidable and durable creature.

Nowadays, if I suggest a woman can't wrestle a 1,500-

pound steer as well as a man, I'm accused of belittling women everywhere and being insensitive to the dreams of all little girls who are being told they can so too grow up and bulldog steers if they want to, and don't let any man say different.

All of that makes this story about the modern typical West Texas woman a little risky in the telling, so I'm resorting to a newspaper trickery we call "The View-With-Alarm Gambit." The way this ploy works is we quote an unnamed source—in this case, a man, and a Yankee to boot—then jump on him for saying offensive things we unequivocally agree with. Most of the time, it works.

I first heard this story at dinner on a floating restaurant in the harbor of Rhodes, Greece, near where once stood one of the world's wonders, the Colossus of Rhodes. This guy began talking about his first marriage, to a Texas woman, and how he escaped north again, where he devised the absolutely perfect definition of a West Texas woman. Drafted into the army, he was sent to Fort Hood to train as a tank driver. One weekend he and his buddies went off to Austin to chase girls. He met his future wife, the daughter of a West Texas rancher who owned twenty sections of land. Instant love. They wanted to wed. The old man didn't like him at all, but they were in love so they ran off and got married. He said he knew life with his new wife would be interesting because she knew more cuss words than he did, and she took her horse on the honeymoon—she liked to ride a little every day.

After the army and graduation, they went to live on the ranch, where he had less status than the sheepherders in distant pastures. He was not a Marlboro Man. The old man put him to digging postholes and stringing barbed wire.

The couple lived in a little ranch cabin, but ate every meal up at the big house. In the next year, he said he had opportunity to study the species of West Texas women, and their ways. "Don't ever let one kick you," he warned. "Those boots are sharp. And don't try to compete with her horse, because you'll lose. A husband is secondary to a horse."

His appraisal of West Texas women was: "They're unpredictable, calculating, argumentative and cross. They will fight you like a man and never forget a slight. They are stubborn and single-minded. You simply cannot beat them. At anything." The West Texas woman, he said, is at home in a country club or beer joint, can drink Lone Star from a bottle or champagne from a magnum, is more comfortable in jeans than dresses and has a vocabulary that would blister a roustabout's ears.

He claimed their marriage was fundamentally flawed from the start. For digging postholes, the old man paid him $100 a month, plus room and board. He was making $100 monthly and she was spending $2,000 on silver-mounted saddles. She had a Neiman's credit card and flew to Houston for parties and things, had memberships in two or three country clubs, and ordered her underwear from France. He said that woman sure knew how to stretch a hundred dollars.

Before long, he wearied of digging postholes, the family was tired of him, he was worn down from competing with his wife's horse for affection. So he fled north, where he described his Lone Star ordeal to friends and came up with the absolutely perfect definition of a West Texas woman. It is this:

"On Saturday night she straightens the Picasso on her living room wall, pats her silver blond hair, takes a final look in the mirror, and then drives in her Mercedes to the

Lubbock Country Club. She is dressed in a $4,000 silver lamé Neiman Marcus dress and an $800 pair of alligator shoes made exclusively for her by a guy in Rome. At the club, she perches herself on a bar stool, crosses her legs, and orders a drink—bourbon with a splash of water.

"Let me tell you something, she is one beautiful creature. The eye of every man in the room is on her. Nothing touches her for poise and beauty. Class, wealth, and breeding, that's her. Then she takes out a solid gold cigarette case from her $500 hand-beaded clutch purse, puts the cigarette to her lips and . . . She'll reach into the purse again, take out a kitchen match, and run the match across her silver lame hip to light it—and that's a West Texas woman."

He said it. I didn't. Shame on him.

West Texas

Tree of

Life

The beginning of West Texas—we are now into mythology—
is a far distance, both geographically and metaphysically, but
arbitrary, and I choose to believe it begins eight miles west of
the county seat town of Palo Pinto beside old U.S. 180, on
the other side of the Brazos River, across a barbed wire fence,
twenty feet into a pasture.

There, two hours west of Fort Worth, is a mesquite
tree—*Prosopis juliflora* in the textbooks, "honey locust" to
early settlers. It is a typical mesquite, twenty feet tall with narrow green leaves and slim curved seed pods. Its trunk, protected by ridged graying bark, is contorted and warped, the
limbs gnarled, studded with two-inch thorns. The mesquite
is an unlovely and menacing tree, a botanical misfit, but it
perfectly defines both the boundaries and character of West
Texas. Where mesquite is, West Texas is.

Quite literally now, West Texas is mythical, the country of
cowboys and oil, hot, windy, dusty, flat—a legendscape of
heroic sweep and scope, and several lies, though the mesquite

is not one of them. Now and then when I drive into West Texas, I stop by to inspect what I have come to believe is my mesquite, to see if somebody has tried to murder it. Someone will, eventually, because in this green epoch of conservation and preservation, the mesquite probably is the only tree man deliberately has attempted to destroy. Man has failed, rather badly.

I selected this mesquite only because I stopped once to inspect an old windmill—another definition of West Texas—in an adjacent pasture and decided to pick some mesquite beans for jelly-making. Sometimes, I drive northwest from my tree to the town of Albany and Fort Griffin, around which grazes the official state herd of Texas Longhorns. These taxpayer heirlooms, living fossils from the nineteenth century, are our brontosaurus, and still another icon and identifier of West Texas. Fort Griffin now is like a prairie Pompeii, but once soldiers went out from there to win the last great Indian wars of the Southern Plains, securing West Texas for settlement, creating a dusty stage for genesis of our American western myth—ranches, the cattle industry, horses, the imperishable cowboy. Mesquite was not intended to be a player in the drama.

The mesquite defines the physical limits of West Texas because it came with the Longhorns herded from their South Texas habitat to the plains. The cattle ate the almost indigestible beans and the beans fell with the droppings, sprouting into trees (or bushes; there are several mesquite varieties). As seen from space, the route of mesquite is a wide band from the Rio Grande Valley curving northwest toward upper New Mexico and Colorado. The botanical mystery is how it survived—it is a semi-tropical plant unsuited to the heat and dryness of West Texas.

But endure and adapt the mesquite has, and man—meaning ranchers and farmers—has attempted for half a century to eradicate it, using fire and bulldozers and chemical defoliants. Not long ago, I passed a pasture of mesquite skeletons—chemical corpses—beside Interstate 20 near Sweetwater. The grayed trunks stood like sentinels, memorials for a lost cause. Science has won only the battle, not the war. Given time, the mesquite will grow there again.

The trouble with mesquite is that it takes water needed for grass and crops. To find water, its roots will reach out laterally sixty to seventy-five feet, and down 100 feet. The beans, eaten green, make cattle sick. The thorns cause infections. The mesquite makes land useless, though the mesquite itself has considerable, and growing, value.

Beyond Big Spring (note how important water is in West Texas, even to the naming of towns), I stopped for lunch at a barbecue joint advertising "We cook with mesquite." The mesquite's dense wood burns hot, and its smoke imparts a particularly savory tang to beef, so much so that lately the selling of mesquite logs and chips has become an $18 million annual business. Gift shops have begun marketing small mesquite items, like bowls and lamp bases, even sculptured pieces by artists because the wood polishes into elegant shades of blacks and reds and yellows. One company manufactures mesquite wood dominoes, another golf club driver heads, still another sturdy frontier-style rocking chairs.

At a roadside fruit stand beyond Pecos, I found jars of mesquite-bean jelly for sale—pectin and sugar and hard boiling produce a delicious spread for buttered hot biscuits. Finely ground into flour, the ripened beans make protein-rich bread or, nineteenth-century settlers wrote, an acceptable—but hardly tasty—substitute for coffee. Pioneer mothers even used mesquite thorn needles to sew rawhide clothing. Its glutinous sap served as glue.

The mesquite survives, and because it does, it has become somewhat of a metaphor for the Texas mythology of individual toughness and tenacity. There even now is an organization—Los Amigos del Mesquite, Friends of the Mesquite—to honor this ugly and onerous tree.

Finally, the mesquite is one other thing necessary to an agricultural land: the ultimate herald and arbitrator of spring, of the growing season. Last March near the ranching community of Guthrie, I paused beside U.S. 82, parking under tall cottonwoods planted a century ago—few trees are native to West Texas. There was a plowed forty-acre field waiting for planting—wheat probably, or perhaps cotton. Mesquite had pushed to the edges of the field. The mesquite leaves had not greened, so I knew the farmer would wait. Other plants might be fooled by a false spring, might bud and then be wiped out by a late freeze, but not the wily mesquite. The greening of mesquite is the first sure sign of spring in West Texas, a fact declared in rhyme by a late Abilene newspaper editor. Annually, he published, as a reminding caution, this poem:

> *We see signs of returning spring ,*
> *The redbird's back and the fie' larks sing,*
> *The ground's plowed up and the creeks run clear,*
> *The onions sprout and the rosebud's near;*
> *And yet they's a point worth thinkin' about—*
> *We note that the old mesquites ain't out.*

Jerry Flemmons

1936-1999

One of Texas' best-known journalists and authors and one of America's most successful travel writers, Jerry Flemmons retired after thirty-two years as a staff member, reporter, columnist, feature writer, and travel editor of the *Fort Worth Star-Telegram*. He had toured the world for more than twenty-five years, traveling to 120 countries for more than two million air and land miles aboard jets and ships, autos and trains, mopeds, horses, camels, elephants, dog sleds, dugout canoes, hot-air balloons, a blimp and one zebra.

Flemmon's stories won most state writing awards and were reprinted in college textbooks. As a news journalist, he covered major international stories: the Kennedy assassination; the Jack Ruby trial; the shootings and murders from atop the University of Texas tower. He was one of six newsmen who served as pallbearers for Lee Harvey Oswald's burial in Fort Worth. He reported from South Vietnam and other Southeast Asia war zones. He once said he spent his life doing what he loved.

Through all his travels, Jerry Flemmons' heart remained in Texas, where he was born, raised, educated, and kept a home base always. Most recently he lived in Granbury, where he was writer-in-residence for Tarleton State University. His death in September 1999 was a loss to Texas journalism and to all who love Texas as passionately as he did.

Flemmons' writing reflects not only his love of Texas but his love of his craft. A journalist who set a standard for his fellow writers, Flemmons filled his essays and columns with sly wit, sharp observations, a clever ability to see similarities in the dissimilar, and occasional bits of honest sentiment. His columns on everything from the fallen angels of a century ago to toy rubber guns and Texas language come from a lifelong habit of thinking about Texas and "things," even while he wasn't writing. Because in his own mind Jerry Flemmons was always writing.